A Spatial Analysis
of Urban Community
Development Policy in
India

GEOGRAPHY AND PUBLIC POLICY RESEARCH STUDIES SERIES

Series Editor: **Dr. John Whitelegg**
Department of Geography, University of Lancaster, Lancashire, England

1. A Spatial Analysis of Urban Community
Development Policy in India
Dr. Derek R. Hall

A Spatial Analysis of Urban Community Development Policy in India

Dr. Derek Hall
Department of Geography and History,
Sunderland Polytechnic, Sunderland, England

RESEARCH STUDIES PRESS
A DIVISION OF JOHN WILEY & SONS LTD
Chichester · New York · Brisbane · Toronto

RESEARCH STUDIES PRESS

Editorial Office:
8 Willian Way, Letchworth, Herts SG6 2HG, England

British Library Cataloguing in Publication Data:

Hall, Derek
    A spatial analysis of urban community development
    policy in India.—(Geography and public policy research
    studies; vol. 1).
    1. City planning—India
    I. Title   II. Series
    309.2′62′0954   HT169.15   80-40952

    ISBN 0 471 27862 9

Printed in the United States of America

Acknowledgements

Grateful thanks are due to Kevin Butler who
drew the maps, and David Orme for the
technical expertise; also to Beverley Cook,
Wendy Hawdon and Hazel Knox for helping with
the typing of earlier drafts. Marina Taylor
typed the final version.

Table of Contents

List of Illustrations

CHAPTER 1

Introduction

1.1 SCOPE AND STRUCTURE

Eighty per cent of India's population lives
in its 550,000 villages. Yet the country's
urban problems are arguably greater than the
rural, if only in quality rather than quantity.
Throughout the earlier part of this century,
India's urban population grew steadily, but
with independence and partition this growth
was magnified particularly in the larger
cities. A number of generally interrelated
reasons can be held responsible for this:
rural-urban migration and the infilling of
the urban vacuum left behind by the departing
British and Muslims; further bureaucratic
growth; industrialisation; relatively high
urban birth rates; refugee in-migration
subsequent upon partition. Although an extreme
example, the growth of Delhi, as the country's
capital and one of the major recipients of
migrant refugees, perhaps best reflects the
combination of all these factors in
contributing to recent urban population growth
(Table 1.1).

The scope of this monograph lies in examining
the spatial expression of responses to such
growth and the problems which have come in its
train. In particular, Indian urban community
development (hereafter UCD) policy is
examined both for the generation of appropriate
conceptual frameworks for analysis and also
for the postulation of future development
directions, calling upon detailed empirical
case study material.

The next chapter (2) thus initiates the
contextual perspective by examining the
processes and nature of Indian urbanisation.
The extent of India's urban growth (2.1) and
the structure of its urban forms (2.2) are
discussed within both a temporal and spatial
framework, emphasising dynamic processes and
the interaction between urban and rural cultures
The administrative framework for urban
planning (2.3) is examined in the light of
the preceding two sections, and discussion is
drawn towards the problem of the Indian urban

Table 1.1.   Delhi's population growth

Year	Total population	%decennial increase
1881	173,393	
1891	192,579	11.06
1901	214,115	11.18
1911	237,944	11.13
1921	304,420	27.94
1931	447,442	46.98
1941	695,686	55.48
1951	1.437,134	106.58
1961	2,359,408	64.17
1971	3,620,950	53.85

Source: Census of India 1971

slum. This provides the focus for the next
chapter (3), which attempts to define and
delineate the phenomenon (3.1). The social
and spatial significance of urban slums, both
in terms of their internal characteristics
and in relation to the wider urban environment,
and indeed within the even larger national
framework, are discussed to reflect the need
for, and potentialities of UDC programmes
in such areas (3.2). While decision makers
may have seen particular factors as being
important in stimulating the need for UCD
policies, the actual administrative response
to urban slums has revealed vast disparities
between on the one hand, need and
availability of authority to meet it, and on
the other hand between the existence of such
authority and the enaction of policies deriving
from it (3.3).

The general contextual frame having been
established, chapter 4 provides a conceptual
examination of the terms and processes
surrounding the enaction of UCD in a self
proclaimed democracy. Discussions of 'community'
within an essentially spatial context (4.1)
tend to revolve around the notions of
territoriality and neighbourhood, and the
relationship with socio-economic and cultural
dimensions. Indian and western experiences
are drawn upon in an attempt to dissect and put
into a working context such semantic ambiguities
The relevance of existing (usually western-
based) conceptual frameworks is discussed
before the more overtly political dimension
of participation and notions of democracy
are explored (4.2). In particular, the
structural role of spatially based voluntary
associations within a democratic socio-
political system is discussed before the
specific concepts of community development and
community action are dissected (4.3). The
differentiation between, and interdependence of
these two terms is viewed within a spatial
perspective which in itself leads on to the
last section of the chapter, and examination
of the role and relevance of area based policies
(4.4).

Reverting to an empirical emphasis, chapter 5
looks at the actual evolution and growth of
UCD in India, focussing firstly on the role
of external agencies, both in the urban and in
earlier rural CD programmes (5.1). The national
urban programme, which was subsequent upon the
earlier stimuli, has been uneven, both in the
distribution of projects under its auspices
and in the relative success or otherwise of
those projects (5.2). This problem is discussed
in relation to the aims and objectives of the
programme (5.3) and the varying importance
given to the role of spatial factors by the
various actors concerned in the UCD process.

Within the national framework, UCD programmes
in three cities are looked at in some detail
Delhi (6.1), Hyderabad (6.2) and Baroda (6.3)

4

with significantly different backgrounds and
approaches, nevertheless present very similar
problems in attempting to enact UCD policies in
specific locations. The detailed empirical
material here presented, together with the
wider discussion previously undertaken, are
brought together in the final chapter (7) for
an overall evaluation of UCD programmes in
India. Thus, having established the spatially
expressed factors, both actual and perceived,
stimulating UCD policy enaction, and having
discussed the aims and nature of these policies,
an evaluation of results so far obtained is
attempted through a constraint framework, which
attempts to mediate between systemic and
conflict interpretations of society to
emphasise the inherent constraints upon policy
enaction (7.1). Reasons for the relative
failure of UCD policy are highlighted by the
constraint framework (7.2), which emphasises
the spatial dimension. In the light of
alternative models for social development,
the geographical implications for public policy
in urban India are set out (7.3). A brief
outline of possible future trends (7.4) is
finally followed by a summary of the conclusions
contained in the monograph.

1.2. OUTLINE OF CONCLUSIONS

The major conclusion arising out of this
monograph thus points to the fact that
because of India's spatially expressed diversity
- at national, urban and neighbourhood levels -
no one policy which is rooted in cultural
values as UCD can hope to be applied with
anything resembling uniformity over the
country's myriad and heterogeneous urban areas.
Although some constraints are universally
present, and operate at a whole range of
hierarchical levels, others are specific to
individual milieux. The three studies reflect
this balance of the universal and specific,
while the constraints themselves - spatial,
social, cultural, administrative, political,
morphological - interact and cross cut to
produce a rich and diverse mosaic of socio-
spatial patterns. That 'community' per se
is not an Indian concept in terms of urban
propinquity (de Souza, 1978) is in itself a
fundamental constraint cutting across spatial,
social and cultural dimensions. That 'community'
is, however, a recognisable concept in
village life does point to the need to more
closely co-ordinate urban and rural
developmental approaches. Today's villager is
potentially tomorrow's urbanite, and while
certainly it can be argued that development
policies should operate effectively to the
ultimate elimination of all rural-urban
migration, in the short term administrative
coordination should be developed between urban
and rural situations to ameliorate the
migrant's socio-spatial transition. But given
the nature of the data base, the level of

existing administrative competence and the sheer
weight of migration, this seems unlikely to take
place.

7

CHAPTER 2
Indian Urbanisation

2.1. URBAN GROWTH

2.1.1. PERSPECTIVE

"How many countries in the world have 148
big cities?" (Bose, 1978,18).

According to India's 1971 census, 'The
world's largest democracy' had a population of
547,949,809 of whom 109,094,309 resided in
places defined as urban, representing 19.9% of
the total. This revealed a 38% increase in
India's urban population since 1961 and of the
39.9 million people this increase represented
19 million, or nearly two thirds could be found
in towns and cities with populations of
100,000 and above (Fig. 2.1 , 2.2).
India's official definition of what
constituted an urban areas was clarified for the
1961 national census. Previously, such a
definition had been left to the discretion of
local authorities, with a consequent disparity
and often lack of comparability between states.
Within the 1961 definition, to successfully
aspire to the ascription of town, any Indian
settlement needed to fulfill four criteria:
an overall population density of over 1,000
persons per square mile; 75% or more of its
working population employed in non-agricultural
occupations; a total population of at least
5,000; the presence of certain urban
characteristics and amenities, such as
industrial areas or areas of tourist importance
(Deshpande and Bhat, 1975,358; Cassen,1978,357).
For the 1971 and subsequent two censuses,
however, a further statistical unit was evolved.
This is the standard urban area (S.U.A.),defined
as the projected growth area of a principal city
or town which is likely to be completely
urbanised by 1991. Thus statistically bounded
units are being utilised for urban purposes in
1971, 1981 and 1991, in stark contrast to the
spatial dynamism of previous definitions (Bose,
1978,62).

8

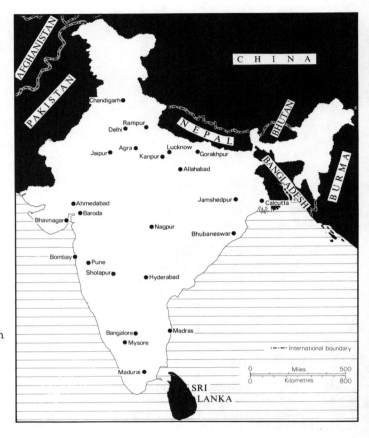

Fig 2.1 Location of major Indian urban centres and other towns mentioned in the text.

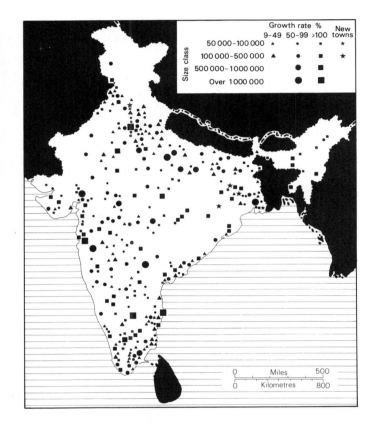

Fig. 2.2 Urban growth 1951–71.

The 1971 national census was undertaken over a period of twenty-four days, from March 10th until April 3rd. (The reference date for the census,however,was sunrise on April 1st). This feat was undertaken by no less than one million enumerators, a fact which in itself presents countless opportunities for computational human error. Yet, as Bose (1978) points out, the first set of provisional tables from the census findings appeared within nine days of the final census date.

Indian census publications do, however, present many constraints on the researcher, only some of which can be alluded to here. In their factorial ecology of six Indian cities, Berry and Spodek (1971) for example pointed to a number of shortcomings in their census material:

(i) census tracts within and between cities often differed widely in size, both in terms of area and population, the latter being particularly significant, ranging from a "few hundred persons" to "tens of thousands";

(ii) data available on a ward areas basis were only available for the first time for the 1951 census, and then only for a limited number of towns and cities;

(iii) usually no maps accompanied the ward data, obviating any possible cartographic expression;

(iv) many occupational data were only available in terms of a vertical industrial basis - for example a sweeper and managing director of the same company would be subsumed within the classification of that company; moreover, the definition of a 'worker' was revised for the 1971 census.

National sample surveys could be a useful means of supplementing the decennial census, and certainly the Planning Commission has sponsored urban socio-economic surveys, but both the N.S.S. and other ad hoc approaches fail to provide anything like a total picture and can be far from accurate. The United Nations (1976) for example, found that the N.S.S. may have underestimated by more than 40% the per capita calorific intake of the state of Kerala. Moreover , such surveys rarely replicate themselves, reducing the possibilities for longitudinal studies on topics not adequately covered by the census or with a temporal grain finer than its own decennial enumerations. Singh (1978) for example found that the most recent N.S.S. material on rural to urban migration was based on 1963-4 survey data, while the 1961 and 1971 censuses employed different concepts to measure migration.

In addition to these shortcomings, since the 1921 census, the Government of India has refused to recognise caste as a characteristic to be enumerated. Yet, despite its official non-existence, caste still permeates urban life as deeply as any other force of social

organisation and differentiation, and
certainly while it is a lessening constraint
on the upper socio-economic and achievement
orientated occupational groups, the absence of
any central enumeration of population caste
characteristics (and hence the need for
individual, restricted surveys) poses severe
handicaps on any Indian socio-spatial analysis.

2.1.2. URBAN GROWTH

In firstly attempting to fit Indian urban
growth into a conceptual framework, Wertheim
(1977) has suggested that there exist perhaps
three basic theoretical approaches to the
spatial nature of urbanisation in developing
societies. The western view, firstly, sees the
diffusion of modernisation from cities and core
areas to the countryside and peripheral areas of
the state. Thus the process of change and
implicitly, the diffusion of urban values,
gradually spreads to the countryside despite
obstinate resistence from an 'inert' peasantry.
Such an elitist interpretation is counter-
balanced by Frank (1969) particularly in
relation to Latin America, where he sees the
dichotomy of town and country in terms of urban
centres acting to reinforce existing 'underdevelopment'. The urban role is not therefore
one of diffusing modernisation, but of
increasing exploitation by acting on behalf of
the distant 'metropoles' of the capitalist
world. In a third approach, the core-periphery
notion has been somewhat inverted by Wertheim.
He claims that the concept is anyway arbitrary
and loose, but in particular, in China it was
the rural core which initiated revolution and
diffused notions of communist development to
overthrow the capitalist urban periphery (the
treaty ports in particluar).

In the case of India, many observers have
pointed to the lack of penetration of urban
values into the countryside, and the apparent
timelessness and permanence of village life.
Indeed the reverse - the transmission of rural
values and economic activities to the town -
characterises large scale (but apparently
declining) rural to urban migration (2.1.).
Certainly a philosophy of development suited
to India's specific needs, was propounded
by such figures as Mahatma Gandi (Ganguli,
1973) and the Bengali poet Rabindranath Tagore
(M.Bose, 1976), but was largely ignored in the
tide of conventional wisdom propelled by
technocratic economists and planners. This was
particularly unfortunate since Gandhi and
Tagore,

"forcefully condemned the urban-industrial
model of the west and had put forward in
concrete terms alternative life styles based
on living in harmony with nature and
development of human resources at the local
level. In particular they drew pointed
attention to the parasitic role of big

Table 2.1 Indian population and urban growth 1901-71

Year	Total population (millions)	Population growth rate	Urban population (millions)	Urban growth rate	Urban per cent of total	No. of million cities
1901	238.34	–	25.85	–	10.84	
1911	252.01	+ 5.73	25.94	+ 0.35	10.29	
1921	251.24	– 0.30	28.09	+ 8.27	11.18	
1931	278.87	+10.99	33.46	+19.12	11.99	
1941	318.54	+14.22	44.15	+31.97	13.86	2
1951	360.95	+13.31	62.44	+41.42	17.30	5
1961	439.07	+21.64	78.93	+26.41	17.98	7
1971	547.95	+24.79	109.09	+38.21	19.91	9

Source: Misra (1978),369.

cities and the enlarging gap between rural and
urban areas" (Bose, 1978, 275).

Lambert (1962) has pointed to each Indian
urban area performing a 'hinge-like function'
in connecting less urbanised areas below it
with larger centres above in "multilevel
hierarchies" of specialisms such as
administration and politics,commerce,religion
and education.
Additionally,

"there is some evidence that many artisans
and small manufacturers, formerly distributed
among the villages, are becoming urbanized, so
that villages must either go into the towns
to get carpentry done, for instance, or must
hire an urban dweller to come to the village
temporarily" (Lambert, 1962, 123).

Table 2.1. gives some indication of India's
urban population growth both in terms of
relative and absolute members during the
twentieth century.
While the general trend is certainly upward
- a slow proportional increase but a very
substantial absolute growth - one or two
qualifications can be made. Firstly, an
obvious hiccup occurred in the decade 1951-61
despite the fact that this was India's most
rapid period of industrial growth. Cassen
(1978) suggests this reflects the role of
perceived or expected earnings acting as a
strong pull-factor in rural to urban migration.
But while past growth may have stimulated such
expectations, these are later disappointed, with
only a slowly adjusting migration pattern
reflecting current economic realities (Cassen,
1978, 121).In this way, a time lag would appear
to have revealed itself: a relatively low 1951-
61 urban growth rate reflecting the poor
economic performance of 1941-51, with the
industrial expansion of 1951-61 not being fully
reflected in decennial urban population growth
figures until 1961-71.
Secondly, in recent years the larger cities
have appeared to grow disproportionately in
relation to, and at the apparent expense of,
the smaller relatively stagnating urban areas.
As table 2.2. shows, enormous growth rates were
recorded for some of India's largest cities in
the 1961-71 period, the nine cities each with
more than a million inhabitants revealing a
total increase of 7.7 million. Thus towns and
cities in the 100,000 range increased their
share of the country's urban population during
this time from 48% to 52%. Towns of 50,000 -
100,000 marginally increased their share of the
urban population; while those smaller than
50,000 showed a relative decline. Indeed at
least since 1951 the revealed trend has been
one of small town stagnation with greatest
growth in the greatest centres (Table 2.3). One
explanation for this (Cassen, 1978,126) is that

Table 2.2. Growth rates above 30% of India's largest
cities 1961-71

	City	1961-71 % growth rate	% employed population	1971 population (millions)	rank size
1.	Delhi	53.9	30.7	3.63	3
2.	Jaipur	52.0	27.0	0.61	13
3.	Jabalpur	45.4	28.9	0.53	16
4.	Hyderabad	44.0	24.3	1.79	5
5.	Greater Bombay	43.8	36.6	5.97	2
6.	Bangalore	43.0	29.6	1.65	6
7.	Madras	42.9	30.0	2.47	4
8.	Pune	42.8	29.2	0.85	10
9.	Ahmedabad	38.1	28.5	1.59	7
10.	Nagpur	34.6	27.1	0.87	9
11.	Kanpur	31.1	30.3	1.27	8
	Calcutta	22.1	32.6	7.01	1

Source : Parthasarathy and Khatu (1978), 9.

Table 2.3 Relative growth of urban size-groups 1901-71

Year	Population of each size-group of towns as a percentage of the total urban population					
	100,000 and over	50,000-99,999	20,000-49,999	10,000-19,999	5,000-9,999	below 5,000
1901	22.93	11.84	16.50	22.06	20.38	6.29
1911	24.19	10.90	17.69	20.46	19.81	6.95
1921	25.31	12.43	16.89	18.91	19.03	7.43
1931	27.37	11.95	18.76	18.97	17.32	5.63
1941	35.40	11.77	17.71	16.29	15.38	3.45
1951	41.77	11.06	16.73	14.02	13.20	3.22
1961	48.37	11.89	18.53	13.03	7.23	0.95
1971	55.83	11.32	16.31	11.32	4.71	0.51

NOTE: 1. From 1901 to 1961 a town group has been classified according to its total population.

2. In 1971, an urban agglomeration has been classified according to its total population.

Source: Bose (1978), 136.

the majority of smaller towns have developed
and remained as market centres with little if
any 'modern sector' activity taking place to
stimulate growth and large scale in-migration.
Certainly all urban centres with populations
of less than two million can be said to be
largely indigenous in terms of character and
growth. Of the four largest cities, only
Delhi exhibits a long history of urban
tradition. Yet until the 1960's, Madras, (in
addition to Bombay and Calcutta) had a larger
population. British influence and the
development of port activities provided the
growth impetus for the three coastal cities,
while Delhi's post-independence mushrooming
has been brought about by a large influx of
refugees consequent upon partition, the
incorporation of surrounding villages within
the municipal boundaries, a proliferation of
central government offices and large scale
industrial development.

Having said that, however, it needs to be
emphasised that the largest agglomeration –
Greater Calcutta – has signified a trend
which is likely to be followed by the next
largest cities. For the 1961-71 period
Calcutta's growth rates were relatively low –
0.7% p.a. for the Municipal Corporation area
and 1.8% for the agglomeration – compared
to 4.4% for Delhi and 5.0% for Madras. Being
fully cognisant of the warning that

"There are few topics on which naive
extrapolation has done so much to damage
understanding as that of urban growth in
developing countries" (Cassen,1978,122-123),

it would seem that as the largest centre,
Calcutta, through congestion, a poor
infrastructure, and particularly bad housing
conditions – has begun to lose its impetus as
an employment centre, with a consequent
falling off in rates of growth. Thus Cassen
(1978) postulates that the currently largest
urban centres will gradually slow down their
growth as new centres take over the impetus
until they too reach a threshold whence they
become too large and congested for continuing
excessive growth. Thus:

"One need not expect either that a large
number of India's cities will reach the size
of some super-megalopolis containing 40 or
50 million people or that unheard-of densities
will be reached....the maximum density of
urban population likely to be reached in India
may already have been experienced in Calcutta.
There is a definite prospect, however, that
vastly increased numbers will be living at
or near this maximum density in various urban
centres as decades of further population
growth go by" (Cassen, 1978,125).

Part of the acceleration in the growth of
urban population from 1961 to 1971 can be
attributed to a more rapid rate of mortality
decline in towns and cities compared with rural
areas, although simultaneously urban birth rates
have also been declining faster than those in
the villages. However, concerned as this
monograph is with urban community development,
it is rural to urban migration while not
necessarily the major component in urban
population growth, is a more socially significant
factor in relation to such problems as social
cohesion and housing provision.

2.1.3 MIGRATION

Urban determinants to migration, apparently
responsible for the slackening growth rate of
India's largest city, have been cited as
including the inability of services and
facilities (such as sanitation and transport)
to take the strain of higher growth together
with factors such as industrial unrest and
general economic difficulties (Bose, 1978,20).
Certainly Cassen (1978,122) has noted the
'push-back' factor wherby the rural-urban
migrant fails to find employment and returns
home. Between 1961 and 1971 the number of
India's internal migrants increased by almost
24% - comparable to the increase in total
population - from 134 million to 166 million.
Of these migrants the rural to urban proportion
increased from 14.5% in 1961 to 15.0% in 1971,
while urban to rural migrants increased
proportionately more, from 3.6% to 4.9% (Cassen
1978,357). Indeed, the revealed long term male
migratory pattern is a move from the village to
town/city in the early years of working life,
with a final return in the late years or on
retirement. Thus Agarwala (1958) has noted
that for males over 40 years of age there is a
tendancy for emigration to exceed immigration.
For Bombay, Zachariah (1966) saw both a
slowing down of rural-urban migration
(600,000 migrants 1951-61 compared with
950,000 1941-51) and evidence of the 'push-
back' effect with apparently insufficient
pull being exerted by the city with the slowing
down of urban employment opportunities(through
industrial decentralisation). Thus 60% of
migrants over 34 years of age returned to the
countryside within four years, and the figure
rose to 76% for those over 65.
While rural to urban migration is apparently
slowing down in the very largest urban
agglomerations, it is certainly of no small
significence, if relatively lower than in many
developing Latin American and African
societies. Despite some attempts at
decentralisation, the volume of migrants has
generally tended to counter balance centrifugal
forces to at least partly produce the Indian
phenomenon of 'over urbanisation', a western
value laden concept expressing the inability

of urban economic growth and services to keep
pace with urban population growth, and an urban
population the size of which cannot be
supported or justified by the country's levels
of agricultural and non-agricultural
productivity (Clinard,1966,73). Indeed, there
are few Indian towns which can generally be
called industrial: Jamshedpur, Kolar City,
Ahmedabad and Kanpur being notable exceptions.
Thus persistent unemployment is found not
only amongst lower socio-economic groups but
also amongst the educated and highly skilled
groups (Malenbaum, 1957).

Although a vast range of conflicting
observations have been made on the subject,
such that

"Almost everything and its opposite seem to
have been observed"(Cassen,1978,120),

Hoselitz (1960) for example has claimed the
push of lack of employment opportunities in the
village has usually been greater than the urban
pull factors claimed by Clinard (1966) to
include industrial employment and wages,
educational, cultural and leisure facilities,
stimulation and anonymity (especially for the
unscheduled and lower caste groups). Implicitly
supporting the primacy of the push factor,
Connell et al (1974) pointed to the fact that
poorer villages tend to stimulate greater urban-
ward migration, especially those villages where
the land is poor and most unequally distributed.
The higher incidence of migrants from larger
families, and particularly the younger sons, has
also been observed, reflecting population
pressure within the village, but particularly
affecting those most likely to be in a position
to respond through migration.

Cassen (1978) however, suggests that migrants
tend not to be from the poorest sections, but
are likely to be relatively educated and
slightly better off, if for no other reason than
they need connections in the city, prospects of
employment and some capital to tide them over
during their resettlement phase after newly
arriving in the urban environment. He suggests
that the very poor, particularly the scheduled
caste groups, have more incentive to leave the
village but fewer prospects of benefitting by
so doing, as they are likely to be discriminated
against when searching for employment, and they
will at the same time, have very little capital
to see them through the settling-in period. Thus
Cassen would appear to be suggesting the
greater importance of pull-factors in this
particular migratory process.

The consequences of such pull factors in terms
of the spatial dimensions of the social and
morphological environment which migrants may
construct themselves, and institutional
responses to them, are discussed in subsequent
chapters.

2.2. URBAN STRUCTURE

2.2.1 MORPHOLOGICAL EVOLUTION

While Sjoberg's (1960) concept of the pre-industrial city has been criticised for its wide ranging spatial and temporal application (e.g. Cox, 1968), such criticism has tended to be epistemological rather than empirical.

In relation to the specifically Indian context, one can trace relatively distinct phases in urban historical evolution, and then analyse the contemporary distinctive landscape features which have evolved through the interplay of cultures expressed in time and space (Fig.2.3). Learmonth (1973) for example, has attempted to discern townscape elements contributing to a descriptive static model of the South Asian city by delineating five major phases in urban evolution.

Ancient Hindu elements firstly, are distinctive, while sharing some characteristics with other phases - the need for defence and administration and the importance of religion. But it is the religious component which is most distinctive here. The form and location of the temple, dominates especially in the south, while the towering spectacle of the temple's large gatehouse (gopuram) adds to the ritual splendour. The temple exerts a strong influence on the townscape, notably in terms of visual impact and use of space, but also in functional attraction of other land uses and residential groups. Thus the bathing lake with its steps (ghats) is usually located adjacent to the temple, whilst the theistic fashionability of the area is likely to attract, or at least retain, relatively high status residence (2.2.4).

Medieval elements, secondly, usually Islamic in character, reveal the relative austerity of the mosque in contrast to the pantheistic nature of the Hindu temple, characterising a period from about the eleventh to the seventeenth century. While defence and administrative functions are pursued much the same way as in the previous phase, Islamic domestic architecture further emphasises the element of purdah. Enclosed courtyards, blank ground level walls facing the street and projecting, screened balconies may all be distinctive morphological symbols of such introspection.

Western pre-industrial elements manifest heterogeneity and differntiation. Heterogeneity in the sense that a central market or several markets may display a wide range of goods, while residential and commercial uses are juxtaposed-shop owners and craftsmen living adjacent to or above their occupational premises. Differentiation is manifested in distinct functional areas - quarters for the production and selling of specific types of goods - cloth, carpets, pottery, jewellery, ironware, cattle, - all dominating particular spatial niches within

20

Fig. 2.3 Morphological model of
        the Indian city

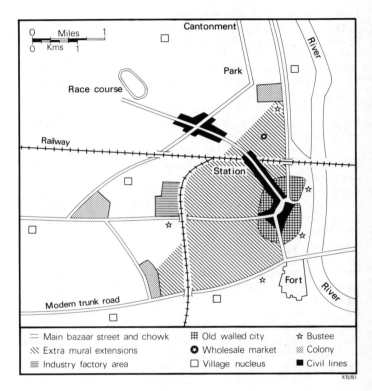

(a) After Smailes (1969), 180.

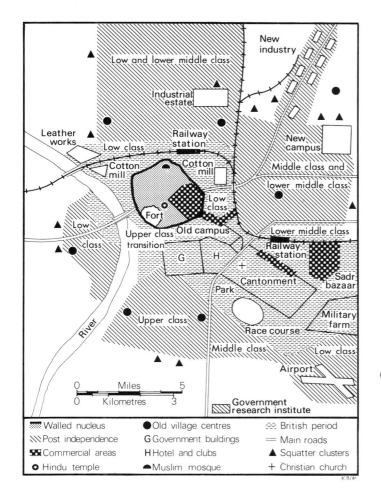

(b) After Johnson (1979), 176.

the urban fabric. Western pre-industrial
groupings have included defensive functions
(Madras' Fort George or Fort William in Calcutta)
usually linked to morphological components
associated with the ports' trade functions. Thus
warehouses and counting houses are particularly
associated with the East India Company's trade
in such high intrinsic value goods as spices
and high quality muslins.

Colonial post-industrial influence was
essentially two-fold, in morphological terms.
On the one hand it developed and transformed
the great port cities — Calcutta, Bombay and
Madras — into modifications of western cities
with high central land values and commercial
development and zonation based upon capitalist
market forces. Indian and European urban
traditions were blended together

"producing a modified kind of European
townscape in which Indo-British culture
evolved and still continues to flourish"
(Brush,1962,58).

In the pre-British urban centres, in such
interior cities as Delhi, Hyderabad and
Bangalore, a duality of townscape arose. Some
distance away from the native city there
developed a distinctly European urban form
characterised by the 'civil lines', the seat of
colonial administration and civil residence,
and the 'cantonment', pursuing a complementary
function for the military.

Forces of industralisation have been
particularly significant since 1947
independence. This has resulted in the further
grafting on of industry to existing urban
centres (a prime example being the development
of such twentieth century industries as
aeronautics and telecommunications at Bangalore)
or the establishment of new industrial towns.
In the latter case, a precedent had already
been established in 1907 with the building of
Jamshedpur — Tatanagar, alongside the steel
complex of the Tata industrial family (Spate
and Learmonth, 1967, 713-715; Keeman.1955).
Since independence further steel towns have been
established with aid from a diverse range of
sources: Durgapur (W.Bengal — British aid),
Rourkela (Orissa — West German) , Bhilai
(Madhya Pradesh — Soviet) and Bokaro (Bihar —
Soviet). Unlike Jamshedpur, however, these
post-independence new towns have yet to show
any significant diversification in their
economic base, little ancillary industry
having been thus far stimulated.

New administrative cities have also arisen
since independence, symbolising rising
political fortunes and attempting to reflect the
dynamically modern approach of the world's
biggest democracy in futuristic city
architecture. Thus Le Corbusier's Chandigarh,
capital city of both Punjab and Haryana states,
and seat of the Panjab University, exemplifies

such implantation in its multi-storey system
built, organically planned layout (Panjabi,
1958; D'Souza, 1968). Bhubaneswar (Orissa) can
be cited as a similar example of a new
administrative city.

Residential segregation on non-traditional
lines has further developed in newly planned
suburbs, but the closely juxtaposed
heterogeneity of Indian urban society has been
further supplemented in recent years by the
vast growth of spontaneous settlements, the
deterioration of the older urban fabric and, in
the largest cities in particular, the incidence
cf pavement dwellers. It is upon these areas
that this monograph later concentrates, and in
the next section the role of such settlements
is seen within a perspective of contemporary
urban morphology (2.2.2.). Subsequently
(chapter 3) 'Urban slums' are focussed upon as
the spatial dimension of the later analyses.

2.2.2. CONTEMPORARY URBAN MORPHOLOGICAL
COMPONENTS

Thus the various historical periods have each
moulded individual Indian cities in relation
to the strength, length and incorporation of
their impress. In terms of the contemporary
scene, however, Misra (1978) recognises four
main forces which go to make up the
'interrelated matrix' of urban land use patterns
:spatial, historical, economic and social :

"In order to understand the structure of land
use of any Indian city and of the million
cities in particular, a few of the existing
notions about land use have to be
re-evaluated and redefined....Land is adapted
to different uses as a consequence of actions
of individuals and groups, primarily motivated
by cultural and economic values" (Misra, 1978,
11).

Karan (1957) analysing the plans of no less
than 832 North Indian towns, and particularly
emphasising the interaction between cultural
forces and physical form, evolved a very basic
morphological classification: elongated (e.g.
Lucknow,Kanpur), influenced by a linear
feature such as a road or river; triangular
(e.g. Dehra Dun, west Uttar Pradesh), related
to some restrictive forces in the site, the
conveyance of roads or a road crossing river;
circular/semi circular (e.g. Meerut,near Delhi),
where a radial street pattern reflects the
influence of the town wall; rectangular (e.g.
Rampur), related to the influence of a
rectangular wall, a fort or through natural
growth at a cross-roads; and finally irregular
patterns not fitting into any of the above
groups but usually related to 'historical
vicissitudes' (e.g. Fatehpur,.near Agra).

In general outline, the indigenous city,
usually surrounded by a wall and penetrated

by relatively few routeways through
fortified gates, is typically less than a mile
in diameter. With closely packed buildings,
heavily residential in character, it possesses
the highest population densities within the
city. While there may be a significant
proportion of non residential land use, for
example Breese (1963) found 41% of old Delhi's
houses put to non residential uses (35% shops,
6% warehouses), little open space will be
available, except in the courtyards of mosques
and temples. This lack of open space is
particularly reflected in the narrow, irregular
nature of the passageways, devoid of pavements
and enroached upon by booths, overhanging
balconies and projecting open shop fronts. The
military/administrative role of the indigenous
settlement is symbolised by the presence of an
historic palace/fort situated by a river or on
a nearby hill within the all embracing battle-
ments and moats, and usually sufficient to
protect the whole population and store supplies
for long periods of seige.

"The pinnacles of Hindu temples and the domes
and minarets of Muslim mosques provide the
distinctive landmarks of the urban profile"
(Smailes, 1969, 181).

and such religious symbols are usually related
to specific neighbourhoods/wards - mohallas -
which may take their names from a variety of
sources, such as the area's predominant caste
or occupational group, the founder's name, or
the pre-existing rural village.
    Within the indigenous city, latter day
British influence is usually restricted to such
symbols of order as the town hall and
municipal offices, an enclosed central market
and a clock tower. While within the main bazaar
- chauk/chowk - and around the distinctive
quarters given over to the areal specialisation
of production and selling, native bankers,
lenders, health practitioners, oculists,
dentists,public letter writers and the like tend
to locate.
    In terms of domestic architecture,Smailes
(1969) has noted the prevalence of buildings
of stone blocks or sun dried bricks (kakaiya)
faced usually with plaster and roofed with
curved tiles. He concludes that the indigenous
Indian city everywhere presents a formless
structure (with the exception of the eighteenth
century planned town of Jaipur). Its
compactness and sharp definition against (what
was) the surrounding countryside reflect the
lack of motorised transport, while extra mural
extensions have reflected not so much
centrifugal expansion as centripetal movement
from outside -

"it is the rural countryside that seeps into
the cities" (Smailes, 1969, 182).

Central business districts as such therefore
hardly exist except in the Indo-British port
cities. This reflects the lack of central
services with low income needs being met in
decentralised bazaars, and the competitive
nature of polynuclear developments in the
former colonial parts of the cities. Brush
(1962) has, however, pointed to retailing
dynamism in the form of accretion of small
shops along main roads, the development of
'self contained cells' (new company towns
and districts) and haphazard infilling of open
spaces in cantonments and civil lines.

The civil lines represented, in morphological
terms, the social, cultural and economic duality
of colonial urban India. Providing for the
administrative and residential functions of
the civil rulers, civil lines were established
in all administrative cities close to, but
a little away from the indigenous city. A
cordon sanitaire visually protected the
contagion (both metaphorically and literally)
of one from the other. Thus in purely pucca
construction they comprised government offices,
a court house, the post and telegraph office,
public gardens, parks and clubs, usually
aligned along a main thoroughfare (the mall).

"Educational institutions were sometimes
sufficiently congregated and extensive to
form a well developed precinct, which may have
expanded into a University area. It was the
usual antecedent of the University in the
Indian sub-continent" (Smailes, 1969, 184).

The bungalows of the colonial officials in
separate gardens with shaded verandahs would be
strung out along tarmacadamed tree-lined roads.
Thus a garden suburb ethos of low density,
landscaped, brick built, predominantly western
architecture typified such areas, contrasting
them strongly with the indigenous city (e.g.
see King, 1976). Since independence, while
some cities' civil lines have been preserved
relatively intact, others, as in Delhi, have
witnessed pucca residential infilling, for
minor Indian officials, interstitial squatting,
demolition and rebuilding in varying
architectural styles and at higher densities.
Many of the functions have remained, simply
changing their administrative character, while
particularly office and warehousing uses have
taken over some former residences - e.g. the
census publications office at 2 Underhill Road,
Delhi. But with outward growth of both the
civil lines and the indigenous city the former
cordon sanitaire has been reduced if not
completely eliminated.

The imperialistic role of the cantonment,
as the working and living area for the colonial
military, is again reflected in morphological
order and an extensive use of space. Of course,
the actual desirability of the residential
area was related to the particular range of

personnell designated to it. While the
earliest cantonments, built for the East India
Company, are more irregular in plan, these
nineteenth century 'plantations' generally
present a formal regularity ranging from the
austerity of lower ranks' barrack blocks to
the officer's residential quarters bearing a
marked resemblance to the civil lines. Since
indpendence such areas have taken on a
variety of residential characteristics.
According to a 1954 survey in Pune for example
(Mehta, 1969), while the cantonment areas of
the city contained 13% of all families, this
resident population was actually made up of 65%
of the city's Jews and Parsees, 48% of the
Christians and only 10% of the Hindus, with
few upper castes but 24% of the depressed
classes.

The third area of direct European
influence was the railway colony, providing
a distinct functional zone in important
railway centres. Here would be developed a
relatively self contained township adjacent
to the main railway station, although literally
on the other side of the track to the
indigenous city, for those employed in the
railway industry. With relatively fewer high
status personnell than either the civil lines
or the cantonment, railway colonies present a
more austere townscape, with regular, grid
plan street patterns and much less planted
greenery. Thus for their time (1870's
onwards) both railway colonies (e.g. Kharagpur,
1900 +, on the Bengal-Nagpur Railway) and
company towns (e.g. Jamshedpur) showed the
greatest morphological regularity coupled with
the highest of functional and social
segregation. But this form of segregation,
involving as it did, the indigenous population,
was innovative in that it involved notions
of segregation and rank based upon economic
criteria rather than caste, regional, religious
or other indigenous characteristics. Thus,
with the highest ranks located furthest from
the centre, such industrial urban forms were
the precursors of socio-economic forces of
segregation which have only extensively
revealed themselves in patterns of residential
location since independence. Thus the picture
which emerges from the colonially influenced
residential areas is one of segregation by a
physical order and formality symbolising the
self perceived integrity of the western
colonialists.

With urban expansion, particularly since
independence, three morphological components
have impressed themselves upon the residential
landscape. Firstly, agricultural villages
have been incorporated into the urban fabric,
consequent upon physical expansion of the
town into the surrounding countryside. Such
villages have largely attempted to retain
their traditional functions and forms, with
the result that they have become significant

urban slums, pockets of poor housing and
minimal facilities often set amongst
relatively fashionable expanding suburbs; or
they may have been converted into market places
for the surrounding urban population.

The growth of spontaneous settlements,secondly
has been stimulated by post-independence
refugee movements, rural to urban migration
and an often deteriorating but increasingly
expensive formal urban housing sector. The
nature and problems of such areas are taken
up in detail in chapter 3.

Suburban growth based upon socio-economic
rather than indigenous forms of segregation
is the third component. While private
exclusively high income suburban housing still
represents a relatively small proportion of
Indian urban housing, the semi-public nature of
housing for government workers, company
workers and various disadvantaged groups is
becoming increasingly significant in the urban
landscape. Thus the residents of such 'colonies'
(e.g. Fig 2.4) usually pay 10% of their income
in rent for the privilege of living in
housing owned by their employers. Indeed with
the shortage of good housing at such
relatively low rentals, a major factor in
employment choice (if choice is available) is
the availability of such company housing.
Outside of the colonies, all rented
accommodation falls within the private sector,
with rents of anything up to 30% or 40% of the
earnings of upper income groups in high status
areas. Owner occupation is ascertained via
private house builders or development
authorities, with loans usually for not more
than five years, available from the government
(if a government employee) or life assurance
companies.

2.2.3 SOCIAL CHARACTERISTICS

Before concentrating upon the discernment of
urban social areas, one can perhaps
point to some patterns which have merged from
analyses of social dimensions at different
scales.

Ahmad(1965) undertook a factor analysis of
the social and economic characteristics of
Indian cities. He discerned that underlying
his 62 variables were basically ten kinds of
differentiation (Ahmad, 1965, 19-21) between
the urban centres. A classification of the
cities based upon such revealed differentiation
can be summarised at a regional scale.

Northern cities can be characterised as
having a low rate of female employment, literacy
and population change, a greater than average
proportion of males and unscheduled castes, a
greater accessibility by railway, small
proportions of immigrants and a low ratio of
employed workers to total population.
suprisingly, southern cities are by contrast
typified by higher rates of female employment,
relatively balanced sex ratios, a higher

28

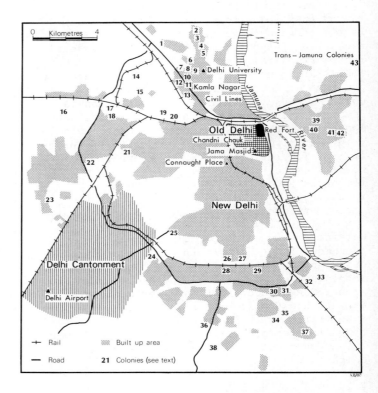

Fig. 2.4 Delhi residential
colonies   .

Key to Fig. 2.4 Delhi residential colonies

1.	Municipal	23.	Delhi Transport
2.	Nirankari	24.	J.J. Colony
3.	Radio	25.	Northern Railway
4.	Dhaka	26.	Civil Aviation
5.	Harijan	27.	Lodi
6.	Delhi Armed Police	28.	I.N.A.
7.	State Bank	29.	Defence
8.	Ishwar	30.	Amar
9.	Gupta	31.	Dayanand
10.	Delhi Transport	32.	Friends
11.	C.C. Colony	33.	New Friends
12.	Delhi Electricity	34.	E.P. Railway
13.	Municipal	35.	Kashmiri
14.	Wazirpur Industrial	36.	I.I.T.
15.	J.J. Colony	37.	Harijan
16.	J.J. Colony	38.	New Jeevan
17.	Electricity	39.	Rajgarh
18.	Bhagwandas	40.	Geeta
19.	Subhadra	41.	New Layalpur
20.	Railway Quarters	42.	Anarkali
21.	Delhi Transport	43.	Nathu
22.	Shardapuri		

proportion of immigrants and of female
immigrants from rural areas, higher rates of
literacy and population, and lower
accessibility to the railway network. Central
cities could be categorised as revealing a
generally low accessibility with heavy internal
concentration upon tertiary activity. Ahmad's
fourth group comprises Calcutta's suburbs,
characterised by a high proportion of males in
the overall population, low rates of female
employment, a heavy concentration upon
manufacturing activity, and relatively high
proportions of employed workers and immigrants.
Finally are grouped together the national
metroplises - Bombay, Calcutta and Delhi (with
perhaps Madras and Hyderabad) together with
other such distinctively individual urban
structures as Kolar and Shillong.

At the city level, both Brush (1968) and
Misra (1978) have discerned general patterns
in population densities. In what may be termed
the traditional cities - the group least
influenced by colonial forces (e.g. Ahmedabad,
Kanpur), - a series of common features have
been recognised. High population densities
within a compact centre in or adjacent to the
bazaar typify this group   (e.g. 136,384 per
square mile in central Aligarh; 136,536 in Old
Delhi) although signs of decentralisation have
recently revealed themselves.

"A semblance of a small crater at the centre
appeared during 1961-71" (Misra, 1978, 7),

perhaps reflecting outward migration of
formally centrally located high status groups
to new suburbs. Within one or two miles of such
centres population densities drop steeply down
to the urban periphery.

A second pattern of population density has
been noted in the British built port-cities -
Calcutta, Bombay, Madras, - in which, due to
the commercially developed centres, relatively
low population densities predominate until, a
mile or so out, density levels increase
dramatically with multistorey, closely packed
dwellings (e.g. Bombay at 873,984 persons
per square mile.) Further out, a gradual decline
in density levels take place, with inevitable
hiccups, over a distance of five miles or more
(e.g. Upper Colaba, Bombay 14,528 per square
mile.)

A third pattern of population densities is
revealed in India's bi - nuclear cities - e.g.
Hyderabad - Secunderabad and Bangalore - where
both the indigenous city and the British
appendage may have similarly high densities
while presenting distinctly separate nuclei.
Such separatism involves the intervening
presence of agricultural land, public parks
and other open spaces, although the nodes are
gradually coalescing.

A final group comprises India's modern
planned cities such as Jamshedpur and

Chandigarh, which present relatively low
population densities throughout, with little
or no concentration in business, industrial or
administrative areas.

As a rider to the foregoing, however, it must
be emphasised that a wide range of dynamic
forces, not least the rapid growth of
spontaneous settelements, can in a very short
time, confound some of the previous statements.

At urban sub-area level, social organisation
can be seen as the complementing component to
social areas. As Friedmann and Wulff (1976)
have pointed out, one cannot naively attempt
to apply western based variables in any analysis
of urban social forces. Social structure,
especially the ascription - achievement
dimension, cultural, particularly religious,
values, and forces of historical development
have evolved an urban social form which needs
to be understood as resulting from the interpenetration of horizontal (kinship, voluntary
organisations) and vertical (occupational,
education, income, caste)dimensions. Friedmann
and Wulff (1976) refer to Germani's (1967)
distinction between social integration -
participation in the wider urban society - and
social adjustment - the ability to perform an
urban role without psychological dislocation -
claiming that Indian social life within the
'neighbourhood enclave' tends to accomplish the
latter while preventing the former. In other
words, spatially expressed residential groupings
are constrained in the social dimension from
further penetrating into and interacting with
other urban socio-spatial structures.

While work by Eames (1970) , for example,
has revealed the importance of urban corporate
groups based upon caste and regional loyalties
buttressing and reinforcing spatial
exclusiveness, one can also point to those
studies (e.g. Bogaert, 1977; Joshi and Joshi,
1976; McGee 1976; Sethuraman, 1976) emphasising
the important role of the informal urban sector
in horizontally extending economic (and
subsequently social) linkages across the urban
canvas. In other studies, it has been suggested
that the whole city may act and think as a
corporate group, as Eames tentatively suggests
from the work of Gillion (1968) on Ahmedabad,
India's 'largest traditional city'. Although
Adhmedabad's walls have long been demolished,
Gillion suggests that they still exist in
residents' minds as symbolic representations of
the city's corporate entity.

The voluntary associationsof upper status
urban groups - exclusive social clubs and
service organisations such as Rotary and Lions
groups perform both a philanthropical role
(see chapter 6 below) and a horizontally, urban
wide integrative function for the socially
and spatially mobile (e.g. see the Caplans'
(1977,1978) work on Madras).

2.2.4 SOCIAL AREAS

If any one conclusion can be drawn from the
myriad studies of Indian urban social areas,
and especially those attempting to construct
a structural model, it is that Indian urban
socio-spatial structure defies modelling. As
alluded to previously, Indian towns' social
structure is often only nominally urban in a
western sense. The spatial heterogeneity
of the Indian urban social scene essentially
reflects two facets of this non-western
structure. Firstly, that residence has not yet
come to serve the symbolic function it does in
developed societies since, secondly, this role
is still largely performed by caste and/or
religion, buttressed, as appropriate, by such
other indigenous dimensions as regional
affiliation, language, occupation and length of
residence. But the nature of traditional social
status and the interdependence and at least
spatial interpenetration of diverse yet
complementary status groups help to produce an
often very obscure patterning of social groups
at the micro-level of analysis. This has
produced often far from equivocal, and sometimes
contradictory, research findings.

Singh and de Souza (1977) have pointed to the
fact that while caste is important in the
rural village for the functioning system upon
which rural social organisation is based, in
urban environments, the meaning of caste becomes
more important in terms of identity rather
than function. Much non-traditional urban
employment simply cannot be subsumed within the
caste system, while the relative annonymity of
the city helps those particularly constrained
by low caste ascription in the rural
environment. Thus many observers have gone to
some lengths to reveal the supplanting of caste
by class in the urban environment:

"Caste and class are antithetical in that the
latter system is said to have a rather high
degree of potential socio-economic mobility
while the former has relatively little. Caste
also is more a village phenomenon than an
urban one since in village societies the
essential base of wealth and power is in only
one sphere, possession of land, while in
cities there are many areas in which a man can
achieve wealth and power. Polymorphous urban
society shakes loose the rigidities of the
caste system " (Berry and Spodek, 1971,352).

Yet in most studies of Indian urban social
structure, caste has been a significant
variable in the spatial distribution of social
groups. As noted above however, because this
role is less strong than in the village, it
is buttressed by the presence of caste
associations, acting as the analogue of
village based corporate groups (Eames, 1970)
and often within the wider urban area (Rudolph,

1960). Thus with the greater complexity of urban life and the difficulty of maintaining caste identity through residential segregation alone, caste groups have become formally organised through their associations, pursuing political and educational roles, and particularly in the south of the country the pursuit of social reform has been witnessed through the amalgamation of non-Brahmanical castes into federations (e.g. the Dravidian Federation).

A second indigenous factor suffusing urban society is that of regional affiliation. Particularly in the more cosmopolitan cities with cultural and linguistic diversity, regional associations develop to extol their culture and language and to partcipate in their own regional festivals if not usually celebrated in the region within which they find themselves. According to Eames (1970) however, membership of these groups is often essentially composed of upper castes and classes, while residential segregation based upon region is not as clear cut as formerly. However, Singh (1968) found in Varanasi segregation of Bengalis, Marathas, other south Indian groups and Brahmans (divided into family based zones). Sen (1960) and Bose (1965) have noted in Calcutta clusters of Rajasthani merchants, Punjabi transport workers, Gujarati merchants together with areas almost exclusively inhabited by Muslims. In respect of Calcutta, Eames (1970) points to the symbiotic relationship between space and culture. He discerns that not only caste and regional affiliations, but also the intersecting dimension of economic and occupational class are all contributing to residential segregation

"Although the neighbourhoods which result are not corporate groups in the sense in which we have defined them, such neighbourhoods are the source for the development of the corporate groups" (Eames, 1970, 179).

Thus Mukerjee and Singh (1961) found a high proportion of mohallas in Lucknow dominated by a single caste, region or religious group, while Majumdar (1960) also perceived neighbourhood stratification by both caste and class for Kanpur as well as Lucknow. Gist's (1957) work on the 1941 census for Bangalore revealed a widespread distribution of low caste groups − only five census districts having no low-caste residents − but with a concentration on or near the city's periphery. At the other end of the caste spectrum, fourteen census districts contained less than 1% Brahmans, while four districts each comprised more than 50%. Gist also discerned four concentrations of Muslims, most representing extreme congestion, while in Delhi the 1971 census revealed 243,5000 of the city's 263,000 Muslims living in Old Delhi or within three miles of it.

Since independence , data on a smaller scale

have been made available (as noted above, 2.1.1)
and these, often supplemented by specific sample
surveys have produced a plethora of urban socio-
spatial analyses. Again contradiction and
paradox in some of the findings is evident. But
at the risk of oversimplification, the major
observed patterns can perhaps be summarised as
follows.

High status residential location close to
city centres has persisted as a reflection of
indigenous cultural forces. Berry and Spodek
(1971) found central high status zones in
Ahmedabad, Bombay, Madras, Pune and
Sholapur. While for the first three cities
at least some measure of socio-economic forces
was evident, Sholapur revealed

"communal status rather than socio-economic
status as the most significant variable in
residence patterns.... Sholapur remains as
testimony of the power of caste and communal
factors in the formation of neighbourhood in
a modern Indian industrial city" (Berry and
Spodek, 1971, 364).

Such dimensions have also been revealed for
Delhi (Brush, 1975; Bopegamage, 1957; Yadav,
1976), Hyderabad (Alam, 1969; Alam and Khan,
1972; Khan, 1978a, 1978b) and Bangalore (Rao
and Tewari, 1976; 1978).In Pune,upper caste
groups benefit from central location in that
it makes separation of residence and workplace
minimal for those who can afford high land
prices; it provides security in times of unrest
and violence in the countryside; and it simply
enables residents to enjoy what the city has to
offer (Mehta, 1968).

High status peripheral suburban developments
have arisen based upon socio-economic class
dimensions and occupation and income.

"Among the highly educated, those engaged in
the highest status occupations, and the very
rich, choice of residential location may
become highly independent of caste" (Mehta,
1969, 507).

Such a trend, contrasting with certral high
status essentially caste based locations, has
been reflected in Alam (1965,1969), and Khan's
(1978a,1978b; Alam and Khan, 1972) work on
the twin cities of Hyderabad - Secunderabad and
has been revealed by Brush's (1975) research
on Delhi and Bombay. With rapid growth in the
city of Gorakhpur during the 1951-61 period
Mukerjee and Singh (1965) discerned the
development of elite group suburbs on the
outskirts there, while Rao and Tewari's (1976)
analysis of Bangalore revealed a similar
phenomenon.

Although far from comprehensive or forming
coherent rings, such patchy high status
suburban developments were noted by Berry and
Spodek (1971) for Bombay and Madras, and for

one outlying ward in Kanpur. Similarly,Mehta
(1968,1969), while recognising the centralised
location of upper caste groups in Pune did note
that (with material dating from 1965):

 "the elite have started to decentralise in
 their choice of residential location" (Mehta,
 1968, 412).

Yet such class based decentralisation saw the
highest income groups moving to the periphery
of Pune city itself rather than to the outskirts
of the wider Greater Pune region. Such residents
tended to be comprised of not only sections of
the old elite who had moved out from the centre
of the city, but also the managerial and
technical elite of the new industries also
located peripherally. Berry and Spodek (1971)
would also add the elite of new institutional,
especially educational, areas locating on urban
peripheries, and tending to be Brahman
dominated.
 Low status outer locations based on either
or both caste and class dimensions have simply
expanded with the urban area, spontaneous
settlements locating on each successive
periphery (3.1) gradually changing their
emphasis from indigenous to socio-economic
criteria, although with continuing large scale
rural to urban migration, the influence of
village life and the cultural forces that
surround it still exert an extremely strong
force in such areas.
 The status dichotomy of centre-periphery is
an historical one, only recently modified by
non-indigenous forces:

 "The social areas underwent change with each
 change in the urban economy and spatial
 structure of activities. The wealthier and
 higher caste people concentrated in the city
 centre, pushing weaker sections and lower
 castes to the outskirts" (Misra, 1978,10).

 Although discussed in the next chapter, the
slum nature of most if not all low status
housing, and its relationship in space with
cultural factors can be noted here. Very
generally of two types - inner urban tenements
and outer zone spontaneous settlements - slum
areas present technical, social and moral
dilemmas to urban authorities (3.3). Twenty two
million people, or over 20% of India's urban
population live in officially designated slums,
and for the four largest cities this proportion
rises to a third. But symbolic of the high
density overcrowding endemic in such areas,
they occupy only 6-10% of the urban land area.
Higher proportions of children, men and lower
caste groups typify slums. In Delhi for example,
while lower castes comprise 14% of the total
population, they make up 65% of the squatter
population. Problems of health and welfare,
employment and income, education, social

organisation and apathy within such areas are
discussed in chapter 3.

What multivariate analyses have been so far
undertaken on Indian cities' social patterns
have usually been by westerners with the
(inevitable?) one eye over the shoulder in the
direction of the Chicago models of urban
structure. Rao and Tewari (1978) for example
present the following summary of analyses
(Table 2.4) from which they conclude that

"neither total rejection nor total acceptance
of the western models is justified..... What
is important is.... the need to recognise
that the Indian city has both metropolitan
and traditional elements and the extraordinary
mix of the elements and scale" (Rao and
Tewari, 1978,27).

As a native of the urban environment that he
analysed for his Ph.D., Yadav (1976) is perhaps
in a better position than most to understand
and evaluate structure, process and patterns
in the Indian city. His micro-level analysis
of the residential patterns of Delhi entailed
the application of a computer to 75 variables,
obtained from the census, sample survey and
such source material as house tax records. He
concluded that,

"Delhi, like many other Indian cities, shows
areal differentiation even at micro level as
indicated by the existence of palatial
buildings and thatched huts. As such the
analytical tools adopted by factorial
ecologists seem to be inappropriate at least
in the case of Delhi: by aggregate analysis
one cannot understand the total reality
existing in the city" (Yadav, 1976, 45-46).

He managed to categorise all Delhi's
housing localities' in terms of their
character and administrative status, (Table 2.5)
and then went on to analyse their spatial
characteristics. Planned high status areas
were seen to locate towards flat high land
(cf. Firey,1947), tending to develop sectorally
but also clustering near nuclei such as
hospitals, a university or employment centres.
Unplanned housing with similar characteristics
clusters together, with regularised unplanned
tending to locate at the urban fringe along a
main road. The temporary unauthorised housing
tends to locate closer to such accretional
features (from which other forms of housing
naturally shy away) as refuse tips, waterlogged
ground and steep slopes, all of which almost by
definition, tend to be peripheral to the urban
core.

Again with one eye cocked in the direction
of Chicago, even Yadav cannot resist the
temptation of seeking descriptive patterns
analogous to some of those of North American
cities. And of course he finds them. Five

Table 2.4

Variation explained by the dimension of socio-economic status in ecological
studies on Indian cities

Study on..	No. of variables taken in the study	Variation explained by socio-economic status/social rank (per cent)
Berry and Spodek (1971):		
Ahmedabad (1961) ..	29	17.4
Bombay (1961) ..	14	29.8
Kanpur (1961) ..	9	35.0
Madras (1961) ..	15	17.6
Pune (1954) ..	19	27.4
Sholapur (1965) ..	33	22.3
Weinstein (1974) :		
Madras (1971) ..	14	22.3
Brush (1975) :		
Delhi (1971) ..	18	17.4
Bombay (1971) ..	18	20.5
Rao and Tewari:		
Bangalore (1974) ..	20	28.0

Note: Year against the city name refers to the reference year of the data
used in the study.

Table 2.5

Categorisation of Delhi's residential areas

A. PLANNED - 37% of total residential localities

1. Government planned

(a) Government quarters developed by the government for its own employees (13 localities).
(b) Rehabilitation localities developed by the Ministry of Rehabilitation to accommodate refugees from Pakistan (25 localities).

2. Private planned

(a) Old planned, pre-independence (15 localities).
(b) Newly planned, post-1947 (26 localities).

B. UNPLANNED - 63% of the total residential localities

1. Authorised unplanned

When building operation is allowed legally by the Municipal Corporation because these localities are the original homes of city dwellers.

(a) Old authorised unplanned - pre-1947:

(i) walled (40 localities)
(ii) extra mural (21 localities).

(b) Urbanised villages - urban villages declared by the Municipal Corporation as part of the main city:

(i) old, pre-1961 (51 localities)
(ii) new, post-1961 (8 localities).

2. Unauthorised unplanned

(a) Regularised unauthorised unplanned-dwellers are the legal owners of the land occupied; declared as a permanent settlement by the Municipal Corporation and dwellers cannot be evicted:

(i) old regularised unauthorised unplanned - declared regularised before 1961 (8 localities)
(ii) newly regularised, unauthorised unplanned, since 1961 (35 localities).

(b) Temporary huts unplanned, unauthorised - no legal ownership titles (20 localities).

Source: Yadav (1976),47-50.

concentric zones can be discerned for Delhi,
interpenetrated by linear development along
main roads producing six or seven (depending
on the reference point)sectors. These "five
distinct zones" comprise a 'pedestrian' zone
of up to two miles from the centre; a mixed
zone of planned and unplanned dwellings between
two and four miles out; a 'regularised' zone
four to five miles from the centre; a zone of
planned localities five to six miles out; and
within a band of six to nine miles from the
centre, a suburban zone of sporadic development.

The one conscious attempt to produce a
conceptual model for the ecological structure
of an Indian city was that of Weinstein's (1974)
work based on Madras. He recognised three
distinctive dimensions as being important
contributions to residential segregation,
dimensions each of which could additionally,
be symbolised and represented by a tangible
phenomenon of the urban fabric. Out of the
influence and interplay of these dimensions, a
theory of residential segregation could be
tested (Fig. 2.5).

Economic functions symbolised by the bazaar
were postulated to induce concentric zones of
desirability along a socio-economic dimension.
A political dimension was represented by
concentric development around the
administrative/political symbol of the fortress.
And thirdly, theistic functions deriving from
the role of the temple stimulated concentric
growth along a prestige dimension. Extending
concepts from the Chicago school, Weinstein
went on to propose:

"The zone of greatest desirability along any
dimension lies closest to the setting
concerned; the zone of second greatest
desirability lies at the greatest distance;
then, from the most distant zone inward,
desirability decreases....The perpendicular
bisector of each side of the triangle
connecting the bazaar, temple and fortress is
distinct because each point on it is
equidistant from a pair of settings. Thus
sectors can be created at various arc-radian
distances on either side of these lines; and
these sectors constitute zones of like
desirability along some dimension associated
with a combination of factors with the
appropriate settings" (Weinstein, 1974, 21).

In short, a centroid represents the optimum
location for accessibility to all three
functions, and thus the optimum in terms of the
highest status factor possible on all three
dimensions together. The optimum location for
two dimensions only will be sectoral,developing
along the perpendicular of the triangle (Fig.
2.5).

While such postulates were only put forward
as propositions to be tested, Weinstein's
application and conclusions were rather weak.

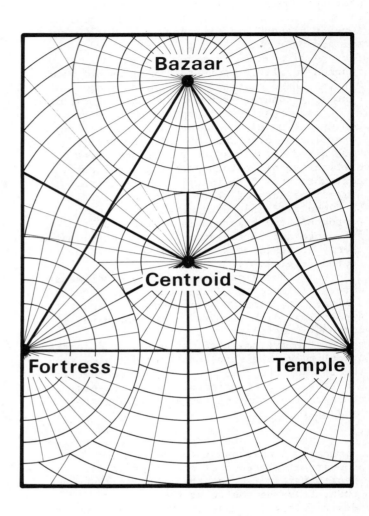

Fig. 2.5 Schematic framework
for a hypothetical Indian city
(after Weinstien, 1974, 23).

A multivariate analysis for Madras
revealed the presence of multiple nuclei, but
between which no clear areal patterns emerged.
The ecological structure of Madras was indeed
declared to share features with the Chicago
models, though in microcosm, but it was
clearly discerned that the temple acted as the
most meaningful focus for the spatial
distribution of social characteristics, with
residence not having replaced or taken up the
symbolic function performed by caste. Thus on
limited data, with a restricted applicability
and an inability to conceptually encompass the
residential status/role dichotomy of centre
and periphery, Weinstein's approach is
acknowledged and passed by.

It is not suprising that Friedmann and Wulff
(1976) are left to declare:

"we lack a heuristic paradigm within the social
sciences that would permit us explicitly to
link these micro-studies with the emerging
paradigms for the study of urbanization as a
macro-process. As a result, we have no
guidelines to help us identify a relevant focus
for research" (Friedmann and Wulff, 1976, 37).

2.3 URBAN ADMINISTRATION

The administration of urban planning in India
first saw the light of day in 1898 in the guise
of the City of Bombay Improvement Act, which,
in the wake of an infestation of bubonic plague
in the city, set up a temporary Board of
Trustees to raise funds, acquire property and
execute works for the purposes of improving the
urban environment. This fin de siècle precedent
was to be followed by sporadic and often very
piecemeal approaches to the ever enlargening
problems of urban planning administration,
problems compounded by India's size,
multiplicity of urban centres and federal
political structure. Inevitably, no uniform
procedures could have been initiated to
incorporate all of urban India. Yet since
independence, with rapid urbanisation
particularly amongst the larger centres,
population growth and attempts at
industrialisation, there has been a markedly
more difficult environment within which to
formalise and enact coherent plans.

Bose suggests a number of reasons for what he
sees as a "remarkable deterioration" (Bose,
1978, 307) in municipal administration:

(i) since independence the country's top
national leaders have been drafted to Parliament
and central government, and to some extent to
the state legislature and governments, to the
detriment and neglect of municipal government
which is "dominated by not always scrupulous
politicians" (Bose, 1978,307), thus producing
at least a degree of nepotism and corruption;

(ii) with the increasing pace of urbanisatior, the demands made upon municipal authorities have greatly increased;

(iii) few attempts have been made to discard the nineteenth century framework of municipal administrative laws and bye-laws, rules and regulations, procedures and practices - the consequence of which is to at least slow down twentieth century processes.

As a result, the variegated approach to urban planning and its administration, as outlined in Table 2.6 for some of India's largest cities, presents, on the one hand, an array of disparate urban and rural local bodies with separate jurisdiction and on the other, a wide range of variously overlapping functional authorities and other agencies controlled and directed by different state level authorities and departments. Thus:

"the approach to the whole issue of governing the metropolis is nowhere near a viable solution. The piecemeal ad hoc measures adopted so far, fail to take a metropolitan view of urban planning and development as well as the maintenance of a delivery system of civic services in a dynamic fast-growing situation" (Raj, 1978,343).

Let us briefly examine a few of the elements in this mosaic. In the absence of precedents, urban improvement trusts, established (apart from Bombay) early this century were usually restricted in scope to the pre-existing municipal authority's boundaries. Seeking to purchase and develop/redevelop land for various urban schemes, flexibility in raising funds saw the Calcutta trust, for example, recouperating money from income generated by improvement schemes together with contributions from Calcutta Corporation of 2% p.a. of the annual value of land and buildings, from a 2% tax on the transfer duty on the registration of properties, a terminal tax on passengers coming into the city and a small levy on jute exported from the port, all in addition to a government grant of Rs 150,000. But such trusts, despite their often elaborate and ingerious sources of revenue raising, generally had no commitment to an overall town planning philosophy, and certainly at that stage there existed neither in reality nor concept a structural framework for operations such as a master plan. Thus at best ad hoc piecemeal schemes were often improvised.

"They had neither the orientation nor the expertise to undertake (the) preparation of comprehensive Master Plans.... The fifties and sixties saw widespread activity in the preparation of Master Plans for cities, which were not generally matched by (the) necessary organisation and administrative infrastructure for their enforcement or implementation" (Raj, 1978,327).

Master plans themselves, as intimated in Table 2.6 have often been imitative, unrealistic and unenforceable. The first plan to actually receive the necessary statutory backing was that of Delhi, and in 1957 the Delhi Development Authority was vested with the appropriate powers to act as custodian of the plan, although direct control was limited to development areas as notified by the government. For other parts of Delhi, a city divided into three local authority areas, the Municipal Corporation of Delhi, New Delhi Municipal Committee, and the Delhi Cantonment Board had responsibility to enforce the master plan and to control and regulate development. Yet, despite the division of responsibilities and powers, the frequent absence of legal powers for appropriate functions, and the almost inherent inertia of Indian bureaucracy, in the fifteen years following the drawing up of the Delhi plan, some 700 other master plans were produced in towns and cities across India.

Often specific planning boards were set up for the formulation of such plans, such as those established in 1967 for Bombay, Pune and Nagpur under provisions of the Maharashtra Regional and Town Planning Act 1966. But after such master plans had been formulated, the planning boards tended to acquiesce and sink into obscurity. The variously constituted local authorities, usually neither properly equipped nor motivationally inclined towards such a task, would be left to take over the responsibility of enforcing the plan and guiding development according to it.

The lack of strategic functions and activities available to local authorities for this purpose eventually led to a spate of legislation in the states in the early 1970's for the establishment of urban development authorities. Arising out of a 1971 conference of ministers for housing and urban development, and aided by a central scheme for integrated urban development, Delhi Development Authority was to a large extent used as a model to follow, although again the powers and roles of the variously emerging bodies often differed quite markedly. Thus Calcutta's Metropolitan Development Authority was not like Delhi's, concerned with guiding a physical land use master plan, but with producing a programme to meet a virtually permanent state of crisis.

This had come about particularly due to what many obervers referred to as a decade of inaction. In 1961 the West Bengal government established a Calcutta Metropolitan Planning Organisation. With the participation of the Ford Foundation (see also section 5.1) a 'basic development plan' to cover the period 1966-1986 was evolved. This was not strictly a master plan but a perspective to guide more detailed

Table 2.6   Developments in urban planning administration
                    in some of India's major cities

1.   AHMEDABAD

     1915 Bombay Town Planning Act declared the municipal
          corporation to be a planning authority.

     1954 Bombay Town Planning Act made provision for
          preparation of city development plans and their
          enforcement by the municipal corporation.

2.   BANGALORE

     1945 Improvement Trust.

     1966 Bangalore City Planning Organisation - special
          agency set up by the government to prepare a
          master plan under provisions of the Karnataka
          Town Planning Act.

     1976 Bangalore Development Authority.

3.   BOMBAY

     1898 Improvement Trust

     1925 Improvement Trust merged with Corporation

     1967 Metropolitan Regional Planning Board

     1975 Metropolitan Regional Development Authority

4.   CALCUTTA

     1911 Improvement Trust

     1961 Metropolitan Planning Organisation Basic Development
          Plan 1966-86

     1970 Metropolitan Development Authority

5.   DELHI

     1919 United Provinces Town Improvement Act extended to
          incorporate Delhi.

     1937 Improvement Trust

     1955-7 Government's Town and Country Planning Organisation
          prepared Master Plan 1962-81

     1957 Delhi Development Authority

Table 2.6. Cont'd

6. HYDERABAD

    1968 State Directorate of Town Planning prepared
    Development Plan – no agency to enforce it or
    law to give it statutory backing.

    1975 Hyderabad Development Authority

7. KANPUR

    1919 Improvement Trust

    1945 Development Board

    1949 Land use and communications plan (with cooperation
    of U.S. planners)

    1959 Development Board merged with Municipal Corporation

    1968 Uttar Pradesh Town and Country Planning Department
    revised 1949 plan

    1973 Uttar Pradesh Development Authorities Act separating
    development powers again.

8. MADRAS

    1920 Town Planning Act

    1949 Improvement Trust, later incorporated into the Tamil
    Nadu Housing Board

    1971 Directorate of Town Planning drew up Metropolitan
    Area Plan 1971-1991

    1973 Madras Metropolitan Development Authority

9. NAGPUR

    1953 Master Plan produced with no legal backing

    1967 Metropolitan Regional Planning Board

IO. PUNE

    1915 As Ahmedabad

    1945 As Ahmedabad

    1967 Pune Metropolitan Regional Planning Board

Source : Raj (1978), 322-340

planning by the Planning Organisation. But
until the CMDA was established in 1970 both

"under a shadow of an extreme crisis" (Raj,
1978, 330)

and under a special statute, little was
achieved.

Coordinating the dispensing of funds to some
58 local development agencies was one of the
CMDA's main tasks, and only if such agencies
fell down in their responsibilities could the
authority step in and carry out such work
itself. On the other hand, the Bombay
Metropolitan Regional Development Authority acts
not only as a planning authority but is also
empowered to revise the regional plan and has
powers of coordination, supervision and
execution of projects as long as these do not
interfere with the jurisdiction of Bombay
Municipal Corporation.

From this structural interdigitation and
functional leap frogging it has been concluded
that

"the establishment of urban development
authorities represents a piecemeal fragmentary
approach without solving and may be, even
adding, to the chaos of subsystems within the
metropolitan area" (Raj, 1978,343).

Such criticism may well be borne out in
section 3.3 below, when discussing the response
of Indian urban authorities to the manifold
problems associated with urban housing. As
chapter six will go on to show, the impact of
urban bodies on neighbourhood structures in the
development of community consciousness and
local environmental improvements varies
markedly both positively and negatively, and
just a handful of case studies in chapter 6
will suffice to reveal, within a spatial
perspective, the wide range of such impacts,
their consequences and significance for the
future.

In concluding this chapter, once can point
to Jones' observation that

"It is a paradox of Indian life that cities
are both profoundly influential and
politically weak...Much of the political
energy contained in Indian cities is not
expended on their behalf as communities but
is instead absorbed in national competition
or on behalf of more specific interets" (Jones
1974, 7).

Bose (1978) suggests a number of root
causes :

(i) planning organisations tend to
concentrate upon the preparation of city
development plans rather than on finding the
necessary financial resources to implement them;

(ii) there is a noticeable and persistent absence of an urban lobby in parliament and the state legislature;

(iii) there is hardly any university in India which offers courses in urban demography or urban economics;

(iv) there exists an obsession with land values within the urban planning process and little attempt is made to reduce land speculation;

(v) residentially, the ruling elite, in their spacious British built bungalows, are completely isolated from the masses.

Thus it is,

"not only the growth of population which is creating severe urban problems but also the lack of a social philosophy for urban development, a callous disregard for the problems of the poor and the craze to construct impressive buildings and showpieces to generate civic pride" (Bose, 1978, 307).

CHAPTER 3
Urban Slums

3.1. DEFINITION AND EXTENT OF THE PROBLEM

3.1.1. DEFINITION

India's Slum Areas Improvement and Clearance Act 1956 (initially established for the Union Territory of Delhi) defines a slum to be:

(i) any area which is or likely to be a source of danger to health, safety or convenience of the public of the area or its neighbourhood, by reason of the area being low lying, insanitary, squalid, overcrowded or otherwise; or

(ii) the buildings in any area, used or intended to be used for human habitation are,

      (a) in any respect unfit for habitation; or

      (b) by reason of dilapidation, over crowding, faulty arrangement and design of such buildings, narrowness or faulty arrangement of streets, lack of ventilation, light or sanitation facilities, or any combination of these factors, detrimental to safety, health or morals.

Within such a wide ranging, yet vague definition vast tracts of urban fabric can be included. Indeed, the entire area of Old Delhi and its adjuncts have been notified under provisions of the 1956 Act as slum areas, containing in 1971 a resident population of no less than 1.3 million.

This is but one reflection of India's state of 'over-urbanization' (Clinard, 1966, 73) industrial and economic development have not kept pace with urbanisation with the result that extensive unemployment pervades the urban scene. Urban services have failed to keep up with population growth such that the economic resources available have not been sufficient to meet the demand placed upon them. Housing shortages, poor upkeep of the housing stock and urban fabric generally, and the increasing cost of living are witnessing not only the

deterioration of existing housing, but the
shift by a large number of residents from high
cost non-slum to relatively low cost slum
housing. Such is the situation particularly
in relation to tenement housing. Spontaneous
settlements (a 'neutral' term employed to
represent those unplanned, self built urban
residential areas variously referred to also as
squatter settlements, shanty towns and hutment
colonies) are again quite another dimension of
the problem, related as they are to such
factors as rural-urban migration, low incomes
and unemployment, and lax planning regulations.

Having relied, at least in the formulation
stage, on western planning models at the
expense of more indigenous and realistic
approaches, Indian urban planners, or at least
their plans, have generally failed to
anticipate the housing needs of a broad section
of urban workers. Thus Singh and de Souza (1977)
while acknowledging the India slum problem as
being shared between tenement housing and
spontaneous settlements, view the requirements
for housing to be located close to employment
as a motivating dimension both increasing
slum development and at the same time
militating against successful relocation of
slum dwellers. They thus recognise four types
of slum: industrial slums, which house the
lower level industrial workers; residential
slums, containing housing domestics and service
workers; construction slums, the usually
temporary housing for construction workers; and
refugee slums particularly numerous in Delhi
and Calcutta following independence and
partition.

3.1.2 EXTENT

While no reliable estimate of the total
number of Indian slum dwellers is available,
partly due to the lack of agreement over the
specific definitional attributes of a slum,
Singh and de Souza 1977 have suggested that
probably more than 20% of India's total urban
population live in slum conditions,
representing some 22 million people, of whom
6.4 million live in Calcutta, Bombay, Delhi and
Madras. Despite such numbers, however, slums -
overcrowded tenements and closely packed
spontaneous settlements - occupy a relatively
small proportion of the urban land area - in
the region of six to ten per cent. Table 3.1
presents what fragmentary statistics are
available on slums per se, while Table 3.2
presents figures purely for spontaneous
settlements.

An additional category is that of pavement
dwellers. While the 1971 census discovered that
0.4% of India's urban population were pavement
dwellers, this figure rose to 0.7% as an
average for the country's four largest cities,
and to 0.99% for Bombay in particular. Such
figures represented a registered growth rate

Table 3.1 Slum dwellers in selected cities

City	Year	No.of Slum Areas	No.of Families	No.of Slum Dwellers	% of total Population
1. Ahmedabad	1960-61	–	18,652	–	–
	1972	–	80.000	789,000	45*
2. Bangalore	1972	159	–	132,000	14*
3. Baroda	1978	192	–	50,000	20*
4. Bombay	1939	85	–	–	–
	1957	144	–	–	–
	1969	206	108,273	613,888	9*
5. Hyderabad	1978	377	–	400,000	20*
6. Madras	1961	548	97,851	412,168	23.8
	1971	1202	163,804	737,531	29.9

*Estimates

Sources: Khatu (1978); Raj (1978); Rao (1978); Rao & Tewari (1976).

Table 3.2 Spontaneous settlements in selected cities

City	Year	Clusters	Households	Population
1. Calcutta	1958-9	28,600	189,000	669,000
	1966	-	-	912,000
2. Delhi	1951	199	12,749	-
	1956	-	22,415	-
	1961	544	42,814	-
	1966	-	77,693	-
	1971	1,124	115,961	1,100,000
	1973	1,373	141,755	-
3. Pune	1937	800	-	-
	1951	6,300	-	-
	1968	17,482	-	-

Sources: Jagmohan (1978); Raj (1978);
           Sivaramakrishnan (1977a); Town Planning Organisation (1973).

of 36% over 1951. In relation to such an
elusive and somewhat emphemeral pursuit as
pavement dwelling, however, such official
figures need to be treated with no small degree
of caution. For example, the 1971 registered
sex ratio of Delhi's pavement dwellers was a
remarkably low 153 females per 1000 males
compared to Madras's ratio of 983, (which was
far above the national average of 930).

Of course, slum problems are hardly confined
to India, although the country is often
exemplified in discussions of the manifold
problems surrounding third world urban housing.
According to United Nations estimates for 1974
for example, while spontaneous settlements alone
accounted for 45% of Bombay's, and 67% of
Calcutta's total population, they comprised even
higher proportions for other developing nations'
cities - 50% Monrovia, 60% Bogota and Ankara,
61% Accra, 72% Santo Domingo, 90% Addis Ababa
(Jagmohan, 1978, 19; see also Karpat, 1976;
Lloyd, 1979).

The insanitary conditions endemic to slum and
especially spontaneous settlement areas derives
from a wide range of socio-economic and physical
factors.

The problem of land tenure almost always hangs
over spontaneous settlements, although the
value laden term 'squatter settlement' is not
always appropriate, as for example in the case
of the (usually) regulated ownership patterns
of Calcutta's 'bustee' areas (see Table 3.3).
Generally, however, there exists the potential
threat of eviction and clearance, whether legal
or otherwise. Additionally illegal, or at least
illicit spontaneous settlement dwellers are
exposed to protection rackets and blackmail,
whether it be the crudely economic and physical,
or the more subtle and sophisticated political.

3.1.3 IN DETAIL

Urban slums, in themselves difficult to
define, are known by different names in
different regions of India, and, not
surprisingly, similarly vary in their
morphological characteristics. Some of the more
common examples are noted in Table 3.3.

In summary, the vast increase in urban slums,
and particularly in spontaneous settlements, can
be attributed to:- high rural to urban migration; high living costs, low living standards
and low expectations commensurate with poverty
and malnutrition; the inability of housing
authorities to meet housing need; insufficiency/
corruption of the local planning system
particularly revealing an inability to eradicate
land use problems stimulating the growth of
spontaneous settlements. Dwyer sees this

"neglect that is usually benign" (Dwyer, 1972,
205)

deriving from five factors militating towards

local authority inaction:

(i)   political powerlessness to reverse the process of spontaneous settlement once it has established itself;

(ii)   constraints on finance available for housing improvement;

(iii) the existence of large tracts of under-used or unoccupied but speculatively held land;

(iv)   the use of physical planning organisations as a vehicle for the dispensation of patronage;

(v)   as indicated earlier (section 2.3) master plans have been promulgated but have rarely been backed by effective enaction, often being steeped in unrealistic and usually irrelevent western-style methodology and jargon.

The spontaneity of such settlements, their unauthorised and unplanned nature, ensure an environment with inadequate or non existant infrastructural services within an urban setting usually already deficient both in such facilities and in the resources needed to obtain and consolidate them. Lack of water, drainage, sewerage, lighting, paving, medical care, formal law enforcement, educational and recreational facilities, together with already low dietary and sanitary standards, overcrowding and flimsy shelter provide a fundamental vicious circle within which rural to urban migrants place themselves. Apathy, village sanitation practices, outdoor community living, the hoarding of any useful article - bits of paper, bottles, string, metal, wood, boxes etc - all contribute to what might be termed a pejorative urban landscape. Yet as shown below (section 3.2) kinship, and other forms of indigenous social control mechanisms are instrumental in preserving and maintaining relative order within this most physically degraded of urban environments.

In a survey of Delhi hutments, Singh (1977, 1978) found very strong social networks operating. Differences in certain aspects of social organisation and culture were found, however, especially in kinship organisation, marriage and to some extent the status of women, these variations being based upon regional origins and caste affiliations. Thus Singh found in her sample that 82% of all single person households were migrants from Uttar Pradesh (who comprised only 24% of total households); that 20% of joint families were amongst the Kahar castes from Madhya Pradesh; while dhobis (laundrymen) from Rajasthan lived in strictly nuclear families. Indeed, 90% of her respondent households were of nuclear families, with the average jhuggi comprising a room of ten by fifteen feet providing shelter, living and storage space for 4.7 people and a couple of goats.

Majumdar (1977) has also pointed to this superficial distinction of nuclear family households and wider group support within slum

Table 3.3   Indian slum names

1. <u>KATRAS</u> : small, single room tenements, generally rows within
   large courtyards or enclosures with a single entrance; often
   Muslim in origin.

2. <u>CHAWLS</u> : multistoreyed single room cubicle tenements particularly
   associated with Bombay.

3. <u>BUSTEES</u> (also Bastis) : a name often liberally given to any Indian
   spontaneous settlement (especially by non-Indians), while deriving
   from a specific land use relationship in Calcutta whereby the land
   belongs to one person, and the huts to another while the actual
   slum dweller is only a tenant paying a monthly rent without any
   claim either to the land or the hut. Otherwise used to denote thick
   clusters of small mud huts with roofs and walls of scraps, wood etc.

4. <u>JOMPRIS</u> : stone and wood huts traditionally associated with Delhi.

5. <u>JUGGIES</u> : another term essentially used in Delhi for wood and straw
   huts.

6. <u>AHATAS</u> : huts built within compounds or walls, and particularly
   characteristic of Kanpur.

7. <u>CHERIS</u> : mud and thatch huts, closely resembling their rural
   counterparts, and typically southern Indian.

<u>Sources</u> : Clinard (1966), Clinard and Chatterjee (1962), Sivaramakrishnan
         (1976).

areas. He discerned core unit groups of 15-25
families linked together by ties of kinship,
caste, village, religious or regional
affinities, although at an individual level
group interaction is based more upon personal
choice. Wider, looser social networks operate on
a more extensive plane, based upon social
homogeneity. Common interest groups are expressed
most formally in associations, which may exist
at local residential, zonal and city levels.
Although only 30% of Majumdar's sample belonged to
such associations, they were seen to be

"gradually emerging as surrogates of kinship,
regional, caste and communal networks"
(Majumdar 1977, 239),

having political, economic and developmental
functions such as slum improvement and
collective security against eviction and
demolition. Perhaps more importantly, the
associations promote structural and functional
links with national institutions through their
provision of an institutional framework to
articulate needs and aspirations of slum
dwellers in relation to the rest of Indian urban
society. Yet,

"It is the remoteness of secular urban
institutions that reinforces the traditional
ties of the basti (sic) settlers" (Majumdar,
1977, 231).

Transition was also seen in terms of group
leadership. Increasingly, those in higher
income groups with better occupational
positions, educational status and longer length
of residence were seen as performing leadership
roles compared to the "grass roots" leaders
drawing their strength from traditional mutual
bonds.
Nevertheless, in the smaller slums of Delhi,
Singh and de Souza (1977) found populations
still dominated by a single caste group, with
segregation based upon caste clusters in larger
and more heterogeneous areas. Indeed, they found
that if slums were demolished, the whole
community was usually relocated together with
residential patterns vis-à-vis other caste
groups not greatly affected. Specifically,
however, the role of caste in urban slums is
seen as a means of identity rather than a
system underlying social organisation as it is
in the rural village.
A lack of appreciation of the subtle structural
and functional relationships between social,
cultural and political processes in slum areas

".... has often led to factionalism, corruption
and failure of many well-intentioned community
development programmes in the past, especially
cooperative ventures which were meant to
actively involve the entire community" (Singh
and de Souza, 1977, 8)

Attempts to improve the physical
infrastructure of slums and particularly
spontaneous settlements, have often been found
wanting because of such misperceptions.

In many ways reiterating the problems found
by Clinard (1966) a decade earlier, Singh (1977)
declared the major physical problem of the
hutments to be : the overloading and poor
maintenance of public latrines presenting
immediate sources of disease; inadequate
quantity and location of handpumps and water
taps needed to supply all water for cooking,
washing, cleaning and bathing; the problems of
public female bathing and the conflict of water
use needs; the lack of covered drains; absence
of electricity and lighting facilities; lack of
security of tenure.

"Throughout India, one is conscious of bodily
functions. A trip through an average Indian
slum area requires considerable attention and
some dexterity to avoid human feces.... In all
slum areas, it is customary for children up to
the age of five or six, and often to the age of
twelve, to defecate in the drains, lanes, or
almost anywhere outside the home. Their
excreta, because of the very high incidence of
disease among them, are the chief means of
spreading such diseases as dysentery and
cholera among the populace" (Clinard, 1966,77).

The presence of cattle, both for religious
and economic reasons, exacerbates the health
problem, for while they consume a great deal of
waste material within slum areas, they
inevitably produce it also. Bombay has achieved
partial success in removing dairy herds from
slum areas and establishing large municipal
dairies outside of the city, but other cities
have been less successful, and holy cattle in
particular remain a distinct, pervading problem.

Water wasteage results in an inadequate
distribution and frequent contamination. Clinard
(1966) for example estimated that 15% of Delhi's
total supply was wasted through public water
taps not being properly turned off or left open,
or plugged with rocks to keep them running
constantly. The taps may also be stolen. Aside
from the illegal breaking open of pipes to gain
access to a water supply, low water supply in
itself can result in contamination. Although
the water is pure in most Indian cities when
leaving the filtering plant, if the supply is
short, the flow must be cut and a vacuum is
created in the pipes, sucking in outside
impurities through weak joints.

Not suprisingly, therefore, while little
adequate data exist on health and nutrition in
Indian slums, those that are available emphasise
the role of environmental factors. According to
Singh and de Souza (1977) the most common
illnesses in descending order, are : respiratory;
gastro-intestinal; dermatological; fever; worms;
ENT diseases; TB and the re-emergence of malaria,

particularly in Delhi. They point out that the slum dweller rarely consults a medical practitioner until the disease has reached an acute state and even then, the high cost of medicines is often such that programmes of treatment are not completed. Thus the patient is re-exposed to infection, a factor apparently doctors rarely take into account. Infant mortality in particular is significantly higher than average, especially for girls, due to a combination of undernutrition of pregnant and lactating mothers, a lack of access to proper antenatal care and large scale malnutrition of under-fives. Thus Singh and de Souza (1977) suggest that the average female slum dweller can expect to lose one child out of every three born. Indeed, in her one year recall health survey in Delhi hutments, Singh (1977) found an overall infant mortality rate of 221 per thousand with young females more likely to die than young males. But caste differences were also notable, the highest rate, at 444 per thousand being found amongst Rajasthani Berwas, a caste in which nearly all the adult females employed are unskilled labourers (see also Sinha and Ranade, 1975).

Such a lack of employment skills reflects the continuity between rural and urban life in the slums, while social networks – particularly caste and regional affiliations – are important in moulding economic perceptions, in regulating the migratory flow finding employment and in helping individuals adjust to city life, they are also 'dysfunctional' (Singh and de Souza, 1977) in limiting social mobility and change within the urban informal sector. This in part at least reflects the underlying social status of slum dwellers. In 1971, members of scheduled castes (chiefly 'untouchables' or 'Harijans' – literally children of God) and scheduled tribes made up 14% of the total Delhi population, but comprised 65% of squatter settlement residents (Town and Country Planning Organisation, 1975).

More needs to be learnt about the precise role of social organisation in employment recruitment mechanisms, the supply of raw materials, market links and credit facilities within the informal sector. Certainly middle men perform an important function in providing most of these, roles which would be beyond the capabilities of slum dwelling workers who are usually paid exploitative wages. Indeed Singh and de Souza (1977) found that, in Delhi at least, half of all slum households spent almost 95% of their income on food and still remained chronically undernourished. Rao and Tewari (1976) discovered a similar figure for Bangalore. Slum dwellers are therefore hardly in a position to consider expending resources on 'better' forms of housing.

It is within this perspective that the later analyses in this monograph are undertaken. As Cassen has recently put it:

"there is a move towards regarding slum
settlements as the only form of shelter the
poor are likely to have and therefore not as
things to be 'cleared', but to be provided with
essential services so that they will be
minimally tolerable" (Cassen, 1978, 127).

Thus Datta (1978) has suggested that a shift
in emphasis of approach from 'housing' to
'shelter' has gradually permeated development
strategies in metropolitan India, being first
realised in planning programmes for Calcutta
(West Bengal, 1966; Kinsley and Kristoff, 1971).
Much slum housing already meets the basic needs
and expectations of the rural migrant. With some
measure of security of tenure, slum dwellers are
themselves able to gradually improve their
structure, thereby investing not insignificant
amounts of 'capital' into this housing form.

3.2. SOCIAL AND SPATIAL SIGNIFICANCE

Majumdar (1977) has pointed to the fact that
rural - urban migrants establishing spontaneous
settlements tend to replicate the physical form
of the village. The initial clustering of such a
settlement is established by small groups of
kin, village fellows, caste and community
members. Subsequent expansion follows further
accretion in relatively compact blocks by
similar groups. For Delhi, a typical settlement
was seen to be composed of 100-150 families,
each with 12-15 metres of space with disputes
rarely arising over different squatter claims
to the same piece of land:

"the spatial configuration that thus evolves
expresses a functional relationship between
social needs and environmental forms"
(Majumdar, 1977, 221/223).

It is under these circumstances that Khatu
(1978) has recognised some thirteen potential
situations whereby slum development can take
place:

(i) in 'configurated areas' of the city,
such as in or near quarries and ravines;

(ii) such linear spaces as railway lines and
yards, open spaces along roads, along old city
walls, parapet walls and footpaths;

(iii) around construction sites;

(iv) adjacent to industrial estates and
complexes;

(v) in and around neglected/disputed
properties or where the owner of a property is
absent;

(vi) open vacant land owned by public bodies
or government agencies;

(vii) agricultural plots within the city
limits, especially around village sites;

(viii) around places of charity, where plots
are owned by trustees;

(ix) on the immediate outskirts of the
city;

(x) abandoned buildings once used for non-
residential purposes;

(xi) old buildings with multiple ownership;

(xii) old villages encompassed by extended
city boundaries;

(xiii) terraces of multistoreyed buildings
in high density or central business areas.

The decisive locational factors for pavement
dwellers — proximity to employment, open yet
defensible space on public or semi-public land -
are similar but more pressing than those for
spontaneous settlements. Thus Singh and de
Souza (1977) recognised two potential types of
site for the congregation of pavement dwellers:
near transport centres (such as railway
stations, bus stations,rickshaw pullins, road
junctions) and commercial centres. The
significance of such dwellers' location in a
limited number of often key areas possesses
important ramifications for the organisation of
such urban dimensions as social services, the
planning of alternative housing and future land
use development.
As previously intimated by the sex ratio
figures, Delhi's pavement dwellers would appear
to be overly male dominated, although in other
major cities the majority live in nuclear family
units:

"they cook,eat,sleep,have intercourse, and die
on the streets...... during the day their
possessions may be stored with nearby people,
but at night fall the sidewalks come alive with
hundreds of cooking-fires and sleeping people
rolled up like mummies in filthy coverings"
(Clinard, 1966,76).

As a number of Indian studies have shown (e.g.
Rao and Tewari, 1976) complemented by evidence
from elsewhere (e.g. Ward, 1976), while
spontaneous settlements appear to locate
primarily for accessibility to employment and
amenities, the potentially least troublesome
site, and that most accessible from the
village, is on the contemporary (and temporary)
urban periphery. Thus with urban expansion
older spontaneous settlements may be seen to be
enjoying the most central and accessible
locations. Certainly evidence from the
Philippines (Ulack, 1978) suggests that
residents in these oldest spontaneous areas

also tend to possess the highest socio-
economic group status. Whether this is related
to length of residence, greater accessibility,
higher area status or other casual factors,
however, is not made explicit.

In spatial terms, Dwyer (1972) has pointed to
the fact that uncontrolled spontaneous
settlements can very rapidly paralyse a city
in three basic ways :

    (i) thay can pre-empt sites which are
required for other purposes;

    (ii) they block off access not only within
themselves but to sites adjacent to them, such
as accessibility to sites on the urban periphery
immediately beyond;

    (iii) they require an extension, reorientation
or redistribution of infrastructural facilities.

But accessibility within such areas, as in
Indian society generally, is reflected in socio-
cultural as well as in spatial dimensions. Singh
(1977) has pointed to the fact that in
spontaneous areas of Delhi at least:

"families of dominant castes clustered together
in such a way as to largely exclude
interaction with minority castes except for the
necessity of sharing public facilities.
Families of minority groups in the basti thus
had little social support and practically no
power of influence in local political matters"
(Singh, 1977, 244).

This may reflect Saxena's (1977) observation
that village migrants tend to come from the
two extreme ends of the socio-economic ladder.
But whereas upper caste groups tend to migrate
to nearby urban centres, lower castes are more
likely to move greater distances to larger
cities. In terms of such a duality, Dasgupta
and Laishley (1975) recognised migrants being
largely composed of, on the one hand, the
relatively highly educated, and on the other,
illiterate, landless labourers.

With urban India's relatively low employment
levels (Table 3.4) reflecting relatively low
overall female employment rates, one is struck
by the vast disparities between urban socio-
economic groups. In Delhi, while it was found
that a mere 5.1% of the city's females were
employed, in the city's spontaneous settlements
the figure was 38.4% (65% of whom were in
construction) (Town and Country Planning
Organisation, 1975). Similarly, in Madras the
respective figures were found to be 6.7% and
30% (Arangannal, 1975). Thus Singh (1978a) has
stated that it is an economic necessity amongst
the urban poor for females in the household to
find some employment, especially as middle age
is approached with the children growing up and
becoming more expensive to support. Sharma

Table 3.4 Urban employment levels, 1971

	Centre	Population	% employed	1961-71 % growth rate
1.	Calcutta	7,005,362	32.6	22.1
2.	Bombay	5,968,546	36.6	43.8
3.	Delhi	3,629,842	30.7	53.9
4.	Madras	2,470,288	30.0	42.9
5.	Hyderabad	1,798,910	24.3	44.0
6.	Bangalore	1,648,232	29.6	43.0
7.	Ahmedabad	1,588,378	28.5	38.1
8.	Kanpur	1,273,016	30.3	31.1
9.	Nagpur	866,144	27.1	34.6
IO.	Pune	853,226	29.2	42.8
11.	Agra	637,785	25.6	25.4
12.	Lucknow	626,246	28.9	26.0
13.	Jaipur	613,144	27.0	52.0
14.	Varanasi	582,915	31.3	19.0
15.	Madurai	548,298	28.4	29.1
16.	Jabalpur	533,751	28.9	45.5
17.	Allahabad	513,997	29.2	19.3

Source : Census of India, 1971

(1975), reflecting the fact that women with the
least education are those most likely to work,
found that 75% of all Indian working females
were employed in just 19 types of occupation.
Apart from the 20% in teaching, nursing and
clerical jobs, the vast majority needed no
education for their work, reflecting the implicit
constraints on girls' access to, and attainment
in formal education. Indeed, in a survey of
21,090 households in 1375 spontaneous
settlements in Delhi, while Majumdar (1977)
found 46% of all adult males illiterate, the
figure for woman unable to read or write was no
less than 90%. Such figures emphasise the
vertical restriction on employment and the fact
that within the informal economic sector, based
upon small scale labour intensive activities
employing adaptive technology, skills are
acquired outside of the formal school system
which would, in the most part, be seen to be
functionally irrelevant anyway.

Buttressed by caste and regional links both
within urban slums and between them and village
origins of the migrants, the occupational
structure of slum dwellers – both male and
female – is tied to an intricate series of
recruitment and friendship networks. In
construction, for example, recruitment may take
place through village based caste and kinship
networks (Bellwinkel, 1973; Lubell, 1977), with
the husband and wife initially recruited as a
team and subsequently segregated into sex-based
work teams for specific jobs.

News of declining employment opportunities in
any urban centre would appear to be transmitted
back to the village relatively quickly (Singh
and de Souza, 1977; although Cassen (1978)
disagrees) thus slowing and/or deflecting
rural-urban migration flows to the urban slums
and avoiding excessive unemployment.
Underemployment, however, remains a major
problem. This in turn will affect urban sex
ratios, which have been levelling out from 845
females per 1000 males in 1961 to 941 in 1971,
reflecting three trends: the increasing
tendency for females to join rural-urban
migration streams; the decreasing phenomenon of
urban women being married back in the village;
and the snowballing effect of more women
bearing children in urban areas (Joshi, 1976).

From a questionnaire survey in four Delhi
slum areas, 81% of women interviewed cited
poverty or some other economic reason for
migrating to a city slum. Family, kinship and
caste considerations were, however, more
important in moulding decisions about migration
destinations both at the city and neighbourhood
levels. But the implicit regional and caste
considerations behind the multi-level
locational decisions of migrant slum residents
have often been poorly understood by resource
allocators, whose perceptions, or rather
misperceptions have been major obstacles to the
successful delivery of social services to the

urban poor (Singh, 1978a).

3.3. ADMINISTRATIVE RESPONSE

Any administrative response to the social and spatial problems of slum dwelling can either come through slum clearance and the development of new housing which, it is hoped (vainly in the case of urban India) will, eradicate the 'slum mentality' ; or perhaps more realistically by accepting the inevitable persistence of slums, and attempting to solve, or at least ameliorate, the social and economic problems, associated with slum living, on a spatial basis. With certain notable exceptions, however, (see below) neither approach has been accorded with significant success.

3.3.1. SOCIAL WELFARE

Under India's federal system, social welfare programmes are statutorily undertaken under state auspices. Most municipal acts, however, assign welfare programmes to urban local bodies, describing them as obligatory or discretionary functions, or subjects to which the municipal fund can be applied (e.g. Madras City Municipal Corporation Act, 1919; Bombay Provincial M.C. Act, 1949; Delhi M.C. Act, 1957).
In order to ascertain the degree to which

"actual conditions do not always correspond to the legal provisions laid down" (Rao, 1972,17),

P.V. Rao undertook a survey of all Indian municipal corporations. In 1971 he sent a questionnaire to the 32 cities concerned to ascertain their actual level of social welfare provision. Only eleven cities (34%) replied, but even these provided a woeful picture of the lack of adequate welfare services provided (Table 3.5). This followed a similar portrait of neglect painted over a decade earlier by the Study Team on Social Welfare of Backward Classes (Renuka Ray Team) of the Committee on Plan Projects. Of 442 municipalities and district boards surveyed in 1959, 293 (66.3%) undertook no welfare schemes whatsoever, while of those which did, over half spent less than five per cent of their total budget on welfare provision. In all cases it was found that level of expenditure bore no relationship to the size of population need.
Raj (1972) pointed to the fact that through structural inadequacies, local government welfare activities, where they existed at all, tended to be handled by the education department or directly by the executive branch of the authority.

"Generally any desire on the part of the municipal council to promote welfare activities finds expression in the form of grants to local institutions and voluntary

agencies...(but)...there is hardly any
purposeful planning....the expenditure lacks
appropriate direction....(such that)....
Voluntary organisations and social work
agencies....have complained bitterly about the
total apathy of the municipal administration
towards the organisation of their activities
to ameliorate and improve the living conditions
of depressed urban communities" (Raj, 1972, 27,
25).

"Our growth-orientated economic planning does
not leave much room for allocation of
substantial funds to welfare programmes....
The only alternative left is, to exhort the
voluntary welfare agencies to undertake the
services with occasional doses of grant-in-aid
from the government" (Bhattacharya, 1972, 32).

The last quoted author is thus left with the
impression that there is a general tendency to
by-pass local municipal government in the
administration of welfare. Welfare Bonds and
State Governments, who it could be argued, are
not in the position to be most locally
sensitive, are often the major agencies
involved. It has also been argued, however, that
welfare should be kept away from municipal
government to depoliticise it. As a consequence
municipal functions have only marginally
expanded, and a local inability to provide for
even the basic civic amenities together with
insensitivity at state level have created a
climate which has witnessed a loss of faith in
municipal institutions.

"The debilitating condition of the latter has
become an excuse for the establishment and
perpetuation of competitive urban local
institutions like Improvement Trusts, Housing
Boards, and Water Supply and Sewerage Boards,
and even taking over of local functions by the
state governments" (Bhattacharya, 1971, 13-14).

Thus voluntary agencies often bear the brunt
of local welfare provision in urban India. yet
Chowdhry (1971, 224) has noted a number of
advantages that voluntary agencies possess over
governmental agencies. These can include
flexibility and ability to experiment; close
proximity to the community and sensitivity to
local problems; ability to foster mutual aid;
utilisation of international charities;
inspiring enthusiasm; ability to act on
controversial matters; and means to raise funds,
whenever necessary, through the community's
participation. The latter role does, however,
pose problems, both in the difficulty of
raising funds and in the unscrupulous manner of
collection and subsequent misuse that some funds
are subject to. It is argued that
municipalities should at least be in a position
to regulate fund raising and to lay down minimum
conditions.

Table 3.5 Selected examples of municipal welfare provision

Welfare services	Municipal Corporations											
	Allaha-bad	Co-chin	Delhi	Indore	Mad-ras	Madu-rai	Nag-pur	Pune	Raipur	Shola-pur	Vara-nasi	TOTAL
1. Poor homes (Beggar homes)	-	+	-	-	+	+	+	+	-	-	-	5
2. Children's homes or creches	-	-	-	-	+	+	-	-	-	-	-	2
3. Relief to the disabled and handicapped	-	-	+	-	-	-	-	-	+	-	-	2
4. Maintenance of lunatic asylums	-	-	-	-	-	-	-	-	-	+	-	1
5. Maintenance of leper homes	-	-	+	-	+	-	-	-	-	+	-	3
6. Maintenance of orphanages	-	-	+	-	-	-	-	-	-	-	-	1
7. Rescue homes for women	-	-	+	-	-	-	-	-	-	-	-	1
8. Care of persons who are infirm, sick or incurable	-	-	+	-	-	-	-	-	-	-	-	1
9. Care for the deaf, dumb and blind.	-	-	+	-	-	-	-	-	-	-	-	1
10. Cash assitance to destitute old persons without means of support	-	-	+	+	+	-	-	-	+	-	-	4
11. Supply of milk to under-nourished needy children attending municipal schools	-	-	+	-	-	-	-	-	-	-	-	1
12. Maternity and child welfare centres	-	+	-	+	-	-	-	-	-	-	-	2
13. Supply of protein with cereal or food to children, expectant and nursing mothers	-	-	-	-	-	+	-	-	-	-	-	1
14. Supply of bread to children under 6 yrs.of age residing in slums	-	-	-	-	-	+	-	-	-	-	-	1

Cont'd.....

Table 3.5 continued

	Allaha-bad	Co-chin	Delhi	Indore	Mad-ras	Madu-rai	Nag-pur	Pune	Raipur	Shola-pur	Vara-nasi	TOTAL
15. Maintenance of Infectious Diseases Hospital	-	+	-	-	-	-	-	-	-	-	-	1
16. Medical aid through dispensaries and maternity homes with reasonable charges	-	-	-	-	-	-	-	-	-	+	-	1
17. Night shelters for pavement dwellers	-	-	+	-	-	-	-	-	-	-	-	1
18. Medical and nursing assistance to poor people in their homes	-	-	-	-	-	-	-	-	-	-	-	0
Total number of programmes for the city	0	3	9	2	4	4	1	1	2	3	0	29

+ service provision
- no service provided

Source : Rao (1972), 18-19

One of the most significant programmes of welfare provision organised by well established voluntary organisations has been that of the Urban Welfare Extension Projects, 85 of which were started in 16 states with grants of R35.2 million but with little cooperation from municipal bodies. Multipurpose welfare services were inaugurated in many urban slums – nurseries, women's craft activities, social education, maternity services and general medical aid – but poor quality staff with a lack of training hampered such an approach (see also Chapter 6). To exemplify such problems, one can cite the Delhi voluntary organisation known as Bharat Sevak Semaj. During India's second five year plan period (1956/7 – 1960/1), together with Delhi Municipal Corporation, this body launched slum welfare pilot schemes for nurseries, school, health and sanitation, recreation and culture, adult education, relief work, family welfare, female work centres, youth and women's clubs (Bharat Sevak Samaj, 1958). In particular, it attempted to establish 49 night shelters for pavement dwellers, but met problems of inadequate staff, (both in quantity and quality), a poor location of shelters (away from the areas inhabited by pavement dwellers and thus missing the point of pavement dwellers' desire to be close to their place of work), a lack of availability of suitable buildings, together with poor co-operation from civic bodies (Chowdhry, 1971).

3.3.2 HOUSING

As one of the multiplicity of agencies involved in housing (Table 3.6, 3.7) local municipal bodies represent a very weak link in the chain of activity.

Slum clearance in particular has suffered from the many structural and moral problems besetting urban India : inadequate legislation, divided and unclear functions, apathetic authorities and slum dwellers, corruption, together with, of course, a vast and continuing physical growth in urban slums and slum populations. In 1952 the federal government launched the Subsidised Scheme of Housing of Industrial Workers, providing a 50% subsidy to local authorities and boards to rehouse industrial workers. This was extended in 1957-8 to cover the rehousing of all slum dwellers. But locally, very inadequate measures were taken. For example, up to 1974 the Maharashtra Housing Board had only built 24,190 units for Bombay, while with 15,000 families being added to Madras' population every year the Tamil Nadu Slum Clearance Board has only managed to construct 16,000 units for that city over five years.

Raj (1978) observes three basic reasons for this 'tardy progress':

(i) the acquisition and clearance of slums is a very slow and difficult process, involving

Table 3.6 Major urban housing agencies in India

National Level   Ministry of Works and Housing

Housing and Urban Development
Corporation (H.U.D.C.O.)

State Level   Housing boards

Housing repairs boards

Slum improvement boards

State industrial development
corporations

Industrial finance corporations

Local Level   Municipal bodies

Private sector

Other local institutes

Source: Parthasarathy & Khatu (1978), 11-12

Table 3.7 Housing/development authorities and complementary
training institutes in India's four largest cities

CITY	AUTHORITIES		TRADING INSTITUTES	
	Nodal	Supportive	Nodal	Supportive
Calcutta	Calcutta Metropolitan Development Authority	Calcutta Corporation; West Bengal Housing Board Municipalities	Indian Institute of Management, Calcutta	Indian Institute of Social Welfare and Business Management, Calcutta
Bombay	Maharashtra Housing and Area Development Authority	Municipal Corporation of Greater Bombay; Bombay Metropolitan Development Authrity; Municipalities	Indian Institute of Management, Ahmedabad	Tata Institute of Social Sciences, Bombay
Madras	Tamil Nadu Slum Clearance Board	Madras Metropolitan Development Authority; Corporation of Madras;Municipalities	Indian Instit of Management, Bangalore	Madras School of Social Work, Madras
Delhi	Municipal Corporation of Delhi	Delhi Development Authority New Delhi Municipality	Indian Institute of Public Administration New Delhi	School of Planning and Architecture, New Delhi

Source : Datta (1978), 10.

"legal hurdles and human considerations" (Raj,
1978, 334).

(ii) finance, technical manpower, materials
and general organisation are far too inadequate
in the face of the enormous tasks needed to meet
an ever growing backlog of housing.

(iii) the cost of construction has so
increased that even subsidised housing is now
beyond the financial means of most slum
dwellers.

For one particular city, the Bombay Buildings
Repairs and Reconstruction Board Act, attempted
to provide a greater impetus to ameliorate
housing conditions. Not until 1972, however, did
the federal Ministry of Works and Housing
announce their Scheme of Environmental
Improvement of Slums. This was a programme for
eleven cities with populations of over 800,000
whereby a grant of R100 per capita was
subsequently extended to a further nine cities
to ensure assistance to at least one major urban
centre in each state. Under the fifth five-year
plan (1974/5 - 1979/80) all urban centres with
populations of over 300,000 have been included
in the scheme, but simultaneously however, in
1974 the onus of the work was transferred to the
rather remote state level with a resultant
decline in activity:

"....success of the Scheme depends greatly on
the motivation, responses and attitudes of the
slum community, which have not been given
adequate recognition" (Raj, 1978, 335).

Outstanding in its exceptional scale and
approach has been the Delhi Development
Authority's handling of slum clearance. Under
the Emergency conditions of Mrs Ghandi's regime,
during the winter of 1975/76 the authority in a
blaze of mixed publicity, cleared and
resettled 400,000 people (80,000 households)
into 27 colonies within six months. The genesis
of this could be seen in the Squatter
Resettlement Scheme sanctioned by the federal
government in 1960 with, initially,
implementation entrusted to the Delhi Municipal
Corporation. The central government, however,
was said not to be satisfied with the DMC's
performance (Jagmohan, 1978) and handed over
responsibility for the implementation of the
Scheme to the Delhi Development Authority, in
1967. As previously noted, the DDA had been
established ten years earlier largely to take
over and expand the purview of the far from
impressively functioning Delhi Improvement
Trust, then twenty years old. With help from the
Town Planning Organisation of the Ministry of
Health, together with a Ford Foundation team,
the DDA prepared a master plan for the city for
the period 1962-1981. Such bureaucratic and
indeed 'western' holistic approaches to long

term problems with the suggestion of
technocratic palliatives, if not total
solutions, was somewhat alien to Indian thinking
particularly at the lower levels. It would
seem that often for example, interests of local
councillors are such that they oppose schemes
which take a long-term view and pose a threat to
their position at the next election. A wider
range of public welfare schemes, particularly
those relating to slum clearance, fail to make
headway due to such inherent deficiencies in the
system forshortening imagination and preventing
long-term and broad views being taken
(Jagmohan, 1975, 110).

Such potential conflict was exemplified in the
now infamous Turkman Gate incident. In April
1976, 6 deaths occured in the process of 120
houses being legally cleared in a scheme
formulated as long ago as 1938. A riot
instigated by 'outsiders' was claimed to be
entirley due to (Sanjay Gandhi's) family
planning campaign and incitement by vested
interests (Jagmohan, 1978, 126).

In Ahmedabad, India's sixth largest city, an
inadequate performance by the Municipal
Corporation in the sphere of housing provision
saw half of the city's 1.8 million population
living in slum areas and squatter settlements,
many subject to protection rackets and

"manipulation by small-time politicians"
(Shah, 1977, 337).

On the other hand the rent of many new slum
replacement tenements had been beyond the
capacity of the people they were meant for, so
that sub-letting was undertaken on a large
scale, with many of the previous slum residents
returning to other slum areas.

This is particularly ironic in a city such as
Ahmedabad, planned, as it was, as a showpiece
by Le Corbusier and Louis Kahn. Indeed one
might almost suggest that it was at least partly
because of the city's initial physical
attractions and improved environment for a
potentially much better social and economic
prospect, that there was so much in-migration
from rural areas. Thus a vicious circle was set
up of an initially well planned city, perceived
as a superior environment and attracting large
scale in-migration sprouting slums and
spontaneous settlements, thereby destroying much
that was attractive to those in-migrants in the
first instance.

In 1972 a slum clearance board was established
for the city. But after a flood swept away
3000 slums and spontaneous settlements,
Ahmedabad's Integrated Urban Development Project
was established, in 1973. A voluntary study
group attached to the project pointed to the
fact that previously when the local authorities
had attempted to drive out squatters, they had
simply returned to their former sites. But the
flooding of such sites had aroused fear amongst

the residents who now wanted to be relocated
within the city.

Involvement of those residents was initially
necessary for any resettlement programme, and a
comprehensive development approach, encompassing
social, economic and political improvements, as
well as housing provision was necessary. For
once, productive inter-agency coordination was
undertaken within the penumbra of the semi-
autonomous project: the state government of
Gujarat allocated a 43 acre site, which although
outside of the city's jurisdiction was provided
with basic infrastructure from the Ahmedabad
Municipal Corporation. The State Government also
provided Rs700 grant per family, OXFAM gave Rs
400 to each family, while the Delhi based
Housing and Urban Development Corporation
(HUDCO) approved, for the residents' housing,
low interest, easy instalment loans. In
addition to the building of the one storey
houses and the necessary infrastructure, the
project's 'social action' component consisted of
soliciting community participation in decision
making; helping to ameliorate the dislocating
effects of relocation; stimulating primary
health and education services; increasing local
earning potential and productive capabilities
by training schemes to improve skills, and
stimulating the development of community
organisation and institutions to promote
residents' self-reliance and self-respect (Shah,
1977). It is this latter point which is
particularly significant, since all project aid
was phased out towards the end of 1978 to allow
residents to manage their own affairs - a
prerequisite for all urban community
development, as will be shown later (chapter 6).
As Datta (1978) has pointed out, however,
establishing training programmes for community
workers who can initiate and then bow out of
such programmes in India is a difficult
proposition in the absence of a stable, well-
structured community development organisation.

Increasingly, relocation programmes are being
looked upon unfavourably. As noted at the end
of section 3.1 above, slum settlements are being
regarded as inescapable, relatively permanent,
and present the only pragmatic approach to
housing the urban poor in such societies as
India. Many would now stress their important
function for ultimate integration into city life
(Ulack, 1978). Yet until very recently, the
hidden costs of slum clearance and redevelopment
were overlooked: the destruction of investment
residents has made in their slums, the greatly
increased transport costs and the loss of
employment opportunities all disappeared under a
tide of conventional wisdom. It is this change
of attitude that has helped stimulate the
process analysed in the following chapters.

CHAPTER 4

Framework for Urban
Community Development

4.1 COMMUNITY

Part of the process of community development
involves stimulating an emotional attachment to
a local area in order that some proprietorial
care and attention will be shown towards that
area. Thus UCD is, in part at least, a spatial
phenomenon, but it is this dimension which also
restricts its wider applicability. By
attempting to draw out the individual
distinctiveness and stimulate a 'community
feeling' in localised areas, differentiation
and potential conflict over the wide urban
fabric is being emphasised. By virtue of the
need to spatially demarcate the 'community'
to be developed, notions of territoriality
are, perhaps inadvertently, brought to the fore.
   Territoriality may be defined as the shared
recognition of, and enactment of behaviour
within, a common area, by self ascribed groups.
Such recognition and attachement to a specific
territory may be structured in a hierarchical
fashion so that people belong to an area which
they feel is part of a larger area. Individual
as well as aggregated group perceptions and
behaviour can also be thus articulated.
Certainly, social psychologists and ethologists
have suggested that space relationships are
perceived and responded to in hierarchical
terms (e.g. Edward Hall's (1959,1968, 1969)
concept of 'proxemics' and the sociolinguistic
parallel in the recognition of a person's use
of 'register'). But are such structurings
innate or acquired? Certainly Fischer and
Baldassare (1975) for example, have suggested
that human territorial behaviour is not
inherited since it is absent in many of man's
primate cousins (Martin,1972; Montague, 1968),
that humans of different cultures vary
considerably in their tolerance of densities
(Hall, 1966) and that dispersion and aggression
patterns among humans are neither seasonal nor
triggered automatically, as they are among
lower animals. It can be suggested, therefore,
that while immediate, personal territoriality

does appear to be an innate phenomenon
inherited by humans, wider territoriality, on a
scale with which this monograph is concerned
appears to be learnt and conditioned by
environmental and cultural factors.

Evidence from the United States such as the
infamous Pruitt-Igoe public building project in
St. Louis (Rainwater, 1966) suggests that class
differences in territoriality reflect the
different functions of the place of residence.
Rainwater discerned that the 'lower class'
concept of home is the provider of shelter and
freedom from immediately external threats.
Conversely, the more privileged classes take
shelter and such freedoms for granted,
collectively identifying their homes as the
symbolic elaborations of a rich social life.
Any environmental threats for these groups only
exist outside of the neighbourhood rather than
just outside the home. Thus is reflected the
territorial distinction between 'lower class'
defensive-instinctive value and 'privileged
class' symbolic-elaborative attributes. Certainly,
despite the cultural dissimilarities, such a
functional/symbolic dichotomy would appear to
hold true in urban India. This is particularly
buttressed in socio-economic and morphological
terms by the 'dual structure' of such cities as
Delhi, Bombay and Madras, whereby the symbolism
of order, regularity and elaboration of the
'colonial' city contrasts quite comprehensively
with the overcrowded, ever-threatened, just-
functioning nature of the indigenous city (e.g.
see King, 1976).

In the Britain which produced such colonial
cities far from its own shore, it was long
held that less mobile urban working class
groups possessed strong territorial identity
expressed in such explicitly territorially
based activities as coronation street parties
(Broady, 1956) and was buttressed and
maintained by homogeneity of the built
environment (Willmot, 1963; Jackson, 1968;
Chapman, 1971; Tarn, 1971) and perhaps a
pattern of matrilocal residence which
maintained a localised kinship system through
the female line (Young and Willmot, 1957;
Townsend, 1963; Toomey, 1970). In this way, it
has been claimed that territoriality has
always held greater pertinence for lower socio-
economic groups, while possessing little
meaning for mobile upper income groups. The
argument thus follows that as man becomes more
mobile the need for territory will become less
important (Webber, 1963, 1964a). This has
particularly far-reaching consequences for
localised urban social planning in the third
world. Doherty (1969) has suggested, however,
that mobility will need to be countered by
stability.

Individual conceptions of territoriality are
both hierarchical and dynamic. They are
hierarchical in that relative importance of
identity can be attached to such categories as

home, street, local area, town, region,
country and beyond. In India, these are further
complicated by religion, in terms of caste or
sect memberhip, by temple or mosque visited
and by rural to urban migration, producing a
rural spatial allegiance for the urban migrant
perhaps far removed in space and culture from
his present resting place.

Territorial images are dynamic in two
respects. Firstly, the relative strength of
identity with any particular hierarchical level
will change according to functional necessity.
For example, territoriality will be expressed
in terms of the home if threatened by
demolition; in terms of a district if buttressed
by caste homogeneity; and in terms of a
region in respect of an area inhabited by
people sharing the same language or dialect.
Secondly, the hierarchy is dynamic in that sizes
and configurations change over time according
to functional circumstances. The 'local area'
may be seen in physical terms as a neighbourhood of homes of similar age, size, material,
lay-out, or as a community of social networks
corresponding with the distribution of local
friends, kin and places of social contact
(taps, communal latrines, etc.). The two need
not necessarily be co-extensive and, indeed,
the spatial expression of social networks can
produce a series of non contiguous spatial
'islands'. Blowers(1973) viewed such
expressions of neighbourhood differentiation
in terms of a continuum, although the present
writer (Hall, 1978) has favoured a matrix
approach as being more amenable for incorporating non-contiguity and non-incrementation.

Neighbourhood, as an entity may well be
moulded according to the conception held by
officials of what it is supposed to represent.
In their preferred visions of territorial
reality, planners may seek to produce 'social
areas' in terms of physical, infrastructural
components. Such an approach was initially
given respectability by the American planner
Clarence Perry who saw the desirability of
setting primary social contacts within a
prescribed spatial context. This relationship
was defined in terms of the size of a population
required to maintain one primary school;
boundaries, to define, separate and articulate
the neighbourhood within the body of the town;
open spaces for recreation; institutional sites,
for educational and social requirements, with
catchment areas as far as possible coincident;
local shops, preferably on the perimeter of
the units; and an internal street system,
related to traffic load and segregated from
peripheral through-traffic routes (Perry, 1929).

Such an emphasis on morphological components,
however, tended to ignore the human factor.
For, while in the west social status is
buttressed and symbolised by a person's/
family's residential accommodation, (the
higher the status the greater being the

symbolic as against the utilitarian value of the dwelling) in India as Weinstein (1974) has pointed out, the role of residence has not yet taken on the symbolic function performed by the caste system, and that social structure in towns and cities is only nominally urban in a western sense. Small scale residential heterogeneity still reflects the interaction between urban location and rural/traditional mores and customs. As yet, little work appears to have been undertaken on the socio-spatial significance of greater physical and social mobility amongst India's growing higher status, suburban based elite. Certainly in the west, mobility further buttresses status distinctions: higher socio-economic groups' social mobility is expressed in residential mobility which generally results in weaker social ties within the residential area compared with lower status areas, and thereby placing greater emphasis upon the physical qualities of residence.

Within relatively homogeneous lower status residential areas, perceived differentiation may rest upon a wide range of often subtly differentiated factors. The closer one is to a group and the more confined the setting, the finer are the status discriminations which are made (McArthur and Long, 1964). In Indian slums the roles of such factors as length of residence; upkeep of dwelling; the way the children are disciplined; the number of children a family has; male occupation and income, may all, superficially at least, bear some relationship to status symbolism in the west (if at times inversely). Such indigenous based roles as position in caste/regional associations, expertise at manipulation in the informal sector, a wife's observance of purdah and strength of contact with village of origin, essentially defy comparison. Yet Keller might almost have been talking about Indian urban socio-spatial differentiation when she noted:

"the boundaries marking off higher from lower residential areas are so minute as to defy recognition by those unacquainted with the local scene. Sometimes only an unmarked path or a single house announces to those in the know the difference between respectability and disreputability..... between having arrived and not quite having made it" (Keller, 1965, 7).

In the British context, Mann (1955) produced a number of polar neighbourhood factors which could be used to analyse any local urban area (Table 4.1)

In her survey of parts of Meerut city in northern India Vatuk (1972) translated the term mohalla as neighbourhood, referring to a bounded and named area of the city. She did, however, draw attention to the fact that

Table 4.1 Bi-polar neighbourhood factors

1. A recognised/unrecognised geographical area.
2. Sparsely/densely populated.
3. Homogeneity/heterogeneity of race.
4. Homogeneity/heterogeneity of culture.
5. Homogeneity/heterogeneity of economic interests.
6. Low/high rate of mobility.
7. Mutual/no mutual help.
8. Neighbours known/ignored.
9. Friendships through proximity/special interests.
10. Local/no local social control
11. Employment within/outside area.
12. No easy/easy escape from restrictions of primary group/to other parts of the city and thus anonymity.
13. 'We'/'me' feeling.

Source : adapted from Mann (1955), 100.

"people speaking of "our mohalla" are
frequently referring to a much smaller area
which constitutes their immediate neighbourhood
within the mohalla as a whole: the alley in
which they live, or a section of the alley set
off by some distinguishing feature" (Vatuk,
1972, 149).

Such a referential definition was seen to be
dependent upon the contextual circumstances and
the breadth of the resident's social contacts.
As

"an egocentrically defined space" (Vatuk, 1972,
150),

such contexts that render the neighbourhood
socially significant vary, not unnaturally,
according to age, sex, length of residence, etc.
The formal mohalla itself generally had greater
significance for women than men. For example,
women living with or near their parents-in-
law observed purdah only within the 'conjugal
mohalla', uncovering their faces once this
socially defined neighbourhood boundary had
been crossed. Buttressed by psychological
barriers, however, Vatuk found in Meerut that
Mohalla boundaries were rarely crossed for
formal social activities or informal visits
except by kinsmen.
   From discussing the concept of neighbourhood,
one inevitably returns to the more nebulous
notion of 'community' and the inter-
relationships between the two. Although often
considered synonymously, Everitt (1976) has
claimed that they are two very different
concepts in that while community is concerned
with human behaviour, neighbourhood is more
spatial, but as we have seen from the above.
Indian example, this is a gross oversimplification. Semantic interchangeability,
particularly in the realm of 'propaganda'
persists, and while it persists, disambiguation
must be undertaken within a perspective of the
value systems which underlie it, since such
'gatekeepers' (Pahl, 1970) as planners and
architects use such terms as if they had a
very real meaning.
   Pessimistically, we can begin with the
opinion that:

"It is doubtful whether the concept 'community'
refers to a useful abstraction" (Stacey, 1969,
134).

In searching for a meaning of 'community',
Hillery (1955) managed to classify some 94
definitions of the concept, this apparent
obfuscation arising from a number of basic yet
interrelated problems which bedevil the use of
'community' at its very appearance. But, if for
no other reason, the very fact that this
monograph is concerned with urban community
development, necessitates some attempt

at dissection and disambiguation.

According to Plant (1974), the use of 'community' operates along two dimensions: the descriptive and the evaluative. Descriptively it has encompassed a wide range of factors, some of which may well be incompatible, while the evaluative, emotive, if not explicitly ideological use of the term is both consciously and unwittingly employed continuously, greatly influencing the selection of its descriptive content (e.g. in propaganda).

Two basic yet competing models have evolved within which to view the community concept. Firstly, the linear development model sets community within the tradition of classical urban sociology, supporting the notion of linear increases in population size and density commensurate with 'progress' from rural-argicultural to urban-industrial society. Tonnies' (1887) and Durkheim's (1933) respective linear transformation concepts of Gesellschaft/ Gemeinschaft and organic solidarity/mechanical solidarity, represent socio-spatial conditions evolving from kin-based, family-structured ties of locality to non-personal, occupation-related structures of friendship and status-based groupings. In this framework there is seen to be a decline in the social significance of the local community per se (Wirth, 1938). But although this approach was reinterpreted in the early expressions of social area analysis (Shevky and Bell, 1955) it fails to acknowledge and explain the extent and forms of contemporary urban community organisation.

The systemic model (Kasarda and Janowitz, 1974) by contrast, questions the assumption that pre-industrial societies were not socially complex, and emphasises that community is a complex system of friendship and kinship ties, and of networks of formal and informal associations, all set in a framework of continuing social change.

A further binary division can be seen as that existing between community as a place-related phenomenon (confused with 'neighbourhood') and as an aspatial or at least 'less-place' (Everitt, 1976) structuring of relationships, attitudes and values. A fundamental prerequisite for 'community' is effective communication. Where the application of telecommunications technology has virtually eliminated most significant space friction, communication is no longer significantly constrained by distance. The role of propinquity declines with 'modernisation'. As well as developments such as the telephone and other telecommunications systems, greater personal mobility has also helped to release the spatial bonds of community. But in all societies to varying degrees, these bonds have only been released for those in the physical, social and economic position to employ the telephone and use the motor car. Such release is still only relative, especially in urban India.

Within the context of increasing urban scale and technical sophistication for communication and movement, conventional wisdom suggests that a decline in locally defined community consciousness should be expected. Implicitly, local activities such as retailing and education may become organisationally polarised, with their operatives living outside of the local area.

Place-related definitions of community have focussed upon two separate facets (Poplin,1972). If a contiguous area is (administratively) designated for a specific purpose, this may help to localise certain functions and aid the potential growth and persistence of a community ('independent territoriality'). On the other hand an area may be dependent upon the community for defining its boundaries ('dependent territoriality'). But even within the realm of a place-related phenomenon, local community, as reflected in residents' cognitive maps, may not be a coherent whole. Rather than expressed as a contiguous area, such a concept may be seen in terms of (isolated) pockets of activity articulated in cartographic terms as a series of islands, such as clusters of culturally similar groups in a spontaneous settlement. Such a pattern is, however, inherently dynamic, and as relationships and activities change their spatial emphasis, so these will be articulated in new spatial terms. Confusion arises when social, psychological and spatial dimensions of such concepts are forced through inappropriate conceptual frameworks. Such confusion can be exemplified by Blowers' use of the concept of a continuum (Blowers, 1973), within which five broad types of neighbourhood were seen - 'arbitrary', 'physical', 'homogeneous', 'functional' and 'community', supposedly ranged horizontally in such a way that each stage introduced a spatial or social dimension of the neighbourhood concept, the dimensions being 'territory', 'environment', 'social group', 'functional interaction' and 'social intercation' respectively. While possessing some merit as an initial classificatory framework, such an approach would also seem to possess an inherent structural weakness (Hall, 1978). As a continuum the concept implies the existence of an aggregative scale -

"as movement along the continuum proceeds so the social dimensions of neighbourhood are introduced until a final stage of social integration is reached...each successive stage incorporates the dimension of that preceding it" (Blowers, 1973, 55, 56).

Yet empirical studies reveal that the dimensions of this contiuum are not ordered, that is any 'stage' does not require the presence of that before it on the scale for its

existence : social interaction - people
enjoying each other's company and deriving some
mutual benefit from it - does not need
functional interaction - common sharing of
shops, community centres etc.- as a
prerequisite; neither necessarily need
homogeneity of social group to be successful,
and so on.

The semantics of community can also be seen to
be misused or at least misappropriated by a
wide range of bodies within the public arena.
For example, while 'community' is used in
contexts where 'successful' interaction is
seen to take place, it is also employed, for
example, by the press, simply as a descriptive
term for where people live, having no
greater meaning than 'place' or 'settlement'.
Confusion and misunderstanding follow when such
use is interpreted as reflecting 'successful'
interactional situations, a consequence not
necessarily unintentional. Indeed Cresswell
(1974) describes the misuse of the term by
certain institutions (e.g. urban development
authorities) as 'propaganda'. In this way,
community

"is one of a number of key words which
themselves embody preferred versions of
reality" (Cresswell, 1974).

Others, he suggests, are 'slum' (see Section
2.1 above) and 'home'.
A final conceptual dichotomy to be examined is
that of consensus and conflict interpretations
of community and society. It has been asserted
that definitions of community entailing notions
of social interaction and shared characteristics
represent a

"consensus model of how the social world should
be, and a pluralist, or at best paternalist
model of how the decision - making process
is carried on" (Bailey, 1975, 83).

Within a conflict model of society, however,
the 'community in deprivation' is the only
possibility, emerging where some common factor
of deprivation - e.g. poverty, famine, flooding,
threat of residential demolition, etc. - unites
it in conflict against those controlling and
distributing resources. The Marxian argument
that class polarisation, and thus conflict, is
inherent in non-socialist society thus views
consensus as the antithesis of conflict, and
stable 'apolitical' communities are seen as
implicit supports to the status quo.
A conceptual framework based upon constraints
rather than conflict or consensus which is taken
up in Chapter 7 to analyse Indian urban
community development attempts a 'realistic'
appraisal of social reality by emphasising the
constraining factors in society which neither
necessarily result in conflict nor consensus. It

tends to follow a wide path of
functionalist anthropological interpretation,
viewing conflict as a process of short-term
change and realignment subsumed within long-
term stability. Within this or any other
conceptual framework, reservations need to be
made in discerning the concept of community as
an actual structural urban entity. The
enumeration of community areas for the purposes
of UCD can only be tentative and relatively
transient in the context of continually
changing city structures; such areas'
cohesiveness will vary considerably, and any
structural analysis imposed from without need
not necessarily correspond to local community
structure as developed and understood from
within. The Indian context calls for the
recognition of an often marked absence of urban
traditions and urban ways of life amongst city
dwellers. Rural immmigrants' attitudes, values
and behaviour patterns may significantly differ
from the 'norm' of conventional wisdom.

"This cultural and behavioural hiatus between
several layers of differerentially urbanised
populace fails to produce the sense of
cohesion, and results in the lack of
integration and a sense of commitment to
improve the quality of urban living. Their
allegiance is primarily to caste or religious
groups rather than to local community"
(Chandra, 1972, 46).

It is the spatial articulation and configuration
(or the lack of them) of such allegiances that
is fundamental to this monograph.

4.2. PARTICIPATION AND DEMOCRACY

Representative and participatory democracy
comprise two conceptual poles, representing
what can be referred to as elitist and
classical philosophical stances respectively,
together with a third, almost midway position,
pluralism.
Mosca (1939) and Pareto (1966) were elitist
theorists who saw political power in society as
the presence of a small homogeneous elite.
Changes came about within such a structure
though a succession of alternative elites rather
than by   large-scale participation. Pluralists,
however, see political power in terms of the
way competing groups are able to exert pressure
on responsive political authorities (e.g. Dahl,
1961). The population as a whole are then not
seen as directly participating in political
processes, but are supposedly exerting
influence through secondary groups. But it can
be argued that secondary groups also become
elitist and oligarchical (Michels, 1958; Kariel,
1966, 1967). In this way, the employment of
professional community workers to aid such
groups has been assessed as simply
'professionalising' such elites and returning

power closer to the hands of officials (Verba, 1961; Potter, 1962; Hendriks, 1972.) Instead of extending participation, it can be argued that the small group system simply distributes elites more widely. Williams (1972) has challenged the notion that wider channels of public participation involve a wider social spectrum of the population in a less stratified structure, since in working class areas, community development agents need to be employed if for no other reason than the fact that residents themselves have insufficient free time.

At the other end of the conceptual spectrum attempted participation by each member of society in every decision making process would produce stagnation and, ultimately, anarchy. The machinery needed for ascertaining such participation, and the processes needed to resolve the resulting conflicting needs and aspirations would be intolerable.

Yet the pursuit of public participation, particularly at the local level, stems from a number of factors: the belief that greater equity in resource allocation can result from the 'planned' themselves being involved in various stages of the process, thereby making planners (and politicians) more aware of their needs and aspirations; that by taking part, the 'planned' may develop a greater feeling of being an integral part of the planning system, and will, thereby, take a greater pride in and show a better appreciation of their own environment; that through a greater awareness of planning procedures and problems, residents will begin to understand the constraints on implementing absolute solutions to problems; that individuals may possess specific talents and expertise which can be called upon; that people know their own needs best; and that human self-realisation or self-fulfilment can be achieved in some measure.

As both a nebulous and overused term , 'participation' can rank alongside 'neighbourhood' and 'community' as terms to avoid were it not for the lack of suitable alternatives. Rowe (1975) has shown that 'participation' subsumes a whole range of attitudes and actions variously impinging upon resource allocating processes which can be viewed incrementally, whereby 'community participation' may be taken to mean: passively listening to the exposition of other people's plans which affect the community; actively helping directly in the making of such plans; helping by proxy or through representatives in the making of plans; actively helping in the execution of such plans, however made; helping indirectly in the execution of such plans; commenting upon the execution of plans; exercising power to obtain changes in plans (especially for resources allocation) made by others; allocating resources; allocating and expending resources (Rowe, 1975).

Total or near total participation by itself,
however, as suggested in these last two
categories, could result in greater
inequalities, producing, as alluded to
previously, virtual anarchy. The economically
and physically strong and active tend to
participate most effectively, leaving the weak
and poor inarticulate and resourceless. Indeed
it can be argued that of the two 'democratic'
extremes, total participation might well
ultimately produce greater inequalities than
elitist representation. In the present context
'participation' thus needs to be viewed within a
set of constraints - relative, rather than
absolute participation being the required goal.
Yet the roles of elected representatives may
be rendered unsatisfactory through the operation
of a number of constraints. A councillor can
attend only a limited number of committees at
which major decisions, often only rubber
stamped in full council, are made, Indian
democracy following the British tradition in
that respect as in many others. Elected members
are often confronted with lengthy documents
upon which they must base decisions without
sufficient time to either read or evaluate what
may well be technically complex reports; neither
are they usually in a position to seek
alternative technical advice from outside of the
local authority. Such représentatives as
committee chairmen, moreover, possess little
time to maintain full commitment to their ward.

In practice the dichotomy of perceptions held
by planners and the planned, and indeed the
often conflicting and cross-cutting variations
of these has produced two stools between which
elected representatives tend to fall. Both at
local and national levels, politicians need,
for electoral purposes, to patronise their
constituents, but at the same time, by reason
of at least self-justification, they give
consent to planning policies whose consequences
they are often far from fully comprehending.
The compartmentalised nature of elected
politicians' perceptions and areas of activity
within the decision making process is further
prescribed by their own individual and group
composition. Thus the effectiveness of
formal political representation at the lower
level is greatly reduced by a series of (often
interrelated) constraint processes.

Local voluntary associations often develop to
reflect viewpoints which are either over-ruled
or ignored by representative authority. They
have been defined as groups possessing five
specific characteristics: formality and a
constitution to give order to group affairs;
voluntary membership; members themselves
defining membership qualifications; group
continuity, and a formal name (Stacey, 1960).

Such organisations can be divided into two
general groups, locality based social
organisations, and pressure groups. Locality
based social organisations can again be divided

into two types. The first may often comprise
community centre based activities. Their
location , number and membership will to some
extent reflect the degree to which the local
authority especially recognises local identity
and interests, and provides facilities and
encouragement for such activities. Secondly,
voluntary social organisations may include sub -
groups not representing values commonly held in
any area. Membership of planned community
centres and allied associations where these
exist may well reflect strong spatial
dimensions, while other types of voluntary
association may be implicitly aspatial.

   Two types of pressure groups can be
delineated; branch or affiliated associations
of national amenity and conservation societies
which, while pursuing a particular ideology,
often subsume several causes, e.g. Indian
Rotary and Lions groups; and secondly, local
action groups which often arise with a single
fixed purpose, usually responding to a
particular perceived external threat to the
local area, such as the demolition of homes in
spontaneous settlements.

   Castles (1967, 2) has referred to the former as
'attitude groups' , acting on the basis of
shared attitudes, and to the latter as 'interest
groups' who are seen to be protecting shared
interests. Attitude groups are notoriously
composed of the more articulate higher income
groups who reside within environments worth
protecting and conserving. It may be the case,
however, that these articulate status groups do
not represent the majority view of an area when
that area also includes elements of low status
housing or squatters' huts. It is the residents
of the latter type of area, the groups found at
the lower end of the socio-economic spectrum
who most need a voice to be raised in their
favour, but who, ironically and almost
implicitly often lack the necessary economic
power, degree of articulateness and political
acumen for such undertakings. Simmie (1971), in
the British context has claimed that leaders of
such activity are likely to be drawn not only
from prfessional groups, but also from
intermediate and unskilled manual occupation
grades, providing groups at opposite ends of
the socio-economic spectrum: a symptom of
inherent social conflicts rather than of
co-operation, class conflict being seen to be
buttressed by resource conflict. Such class
groups seek to influence the distribution of
scarce urban resources through political
activity for the benefit of their particular
areas and members, while forced to compete with
each other for access to the same limited
resources in their attempts to affect the
policies and decisions of local and central
authorities. But in Britain at least it is
often the case that local authorities
incorporate successful voluntary services
themselves; the reverse may be true in many

Indian towns and cities. The local authority
may be vested with certain enabling powers, but
because of shortcomings in finance, personnel
and administrative machinery such functions
may be delegated to local voluntary associations
and private organisations. In both cultural
contexts, however, because voluntary bodies
tend to lack political weight, the council can
consult and co-operate with whichever of them
best suits its interest. If a voluntary body
makes inconvenient demands, the council can
claim that the association has no legitimised
authority to speak for local people.

4.3. COMMUNITY DEVELOPMENT AND COMMUNITY ACTION

These twin concepts tend to reflect, in
empirical terms, consensus and conflict
approaches to community. Community development
suggests a paternalistic approach in that a
community development 'agency' outside of the
resident population acts to 'develop' that
population. This may include promoting
facilities desired by local residents; serving
local community action groups; emphasising and
publicising social injustices; and influencing
local political parties (Holman, 1973a). But
Plant (1974), emphasising the lack of
synonymity between community and locality has
pointed out that by virtue of the fact that
community work is deemed necessary within a
specific locality, locality as such, therefore,
cannot be regarded as a sufficient criterion
for community (Plant, 1974). Neighbourhood
relationships are thus viewed as needing to be
transformed through the infusion of such change
agents as community centres and community
schools.

Community action, although entailing notions
of transformation, emphasises motivation and
action stimulated from within the community,
particularly in the sense of a 'community in
deprivation' acting in conflict with specific
resource allocating agencies. Two different
interpretations of the term have been noted, one
within the conflict approach, but with the other
arising from yet another potential source of
semantic confusion (Bryant, 1972). In the
first, community action makes explicit the
tensions and inequalities which may exist in
various situations. But while such a concept
suggests the underlying role of a territorial
dimension, three factors constrain any co-
extensiveness between community action and
spatial community: community action groups
may not be residentially based; formal political
and administrative power is usually located
outside of residential areas, requiring forms
of extra-territorial action; 'professional
change agents' may be needed for specialist
services (e.g. legal advice) who, by their very
status, are unlikely to reside within the
'community in deprivation' for which they are
acting. The second interpretation of community

action entails any planned attempts to involve
groups in self-help schemes or within formal
processes of 'public participation'. Such use
Bryant (1972) considers deceptive, since the
more general ascription of 'community work' is
also applicable here.

In the strictly Indian context, problems arise
in that the terms and notions of community
development, community action and community work
are often intermixed, transmuted and ultimately
rendered devoid of any specific meaning, by
both indigenous and external observers. Clinard
for example transposes the first two terms when
he claims that urban community development
involves two fundamental ideas: the development
of effective community-feeling within an urban
context; and the development of self-help and
citizen participation in seeking community
integration and change (Clinard, 1966, 116).
is because of the widespread nature of such
semantic imprecision that 'community
development' will be employed in this monograph
as an umbrella term entailing aspects of
'development', 'action' and 'work' in relation
to the 'community'. Implicitly, however, there
is an element of spatial attachment running
through such concepts in this monograph, and
the next section looks specifically at area -
based policies.

4.4. AREA-BASED POLICIES

Arguments against area-based approaches to
urban development problems are wide-ranging. It
has been claimed that for the choice of such
areas, officials may employ what has been
referred to (Duncan, 1974) as the 'inverse-care'
law whereby limited resources are directed to
those areas where official objectives appear
most realisable (Brooks, 1975) rather than to
those areas which may most need them.
Implicitly, area-based policies tend to
discriminate against problems not amenable to
area analysis and solutions, as well as against
those aspects of problems whose origin or major
characteristics fall outside of the prescribed
spatial context (Barnes and Lucas, 1974). Some
area specific approaches to tackling problems,
however, develop upon administratively
convenient assumptions, that the causes of those
problems may be found within the area itself
rather than relating to the wider socio-
political and economic environment in which the
local area finds itself (Hamnett, 1979). Further,
it has been argued that by the time specialised
legislation to deal with particular patterns
of socio-economic stress appears, the original
condition stimulating the need for such
intervention may have changed, such as dynamic
causal factors contributing to local
unemployment or ill health, even if the
stressful results persist. Throughout, boundary
delimitation for such areas provides problems
in terms of establishing relatively homogeneous

areas whose internal characteristics and service functions are spatially co-terminous. For example, while 'deprivation' may reveal characteristics which are not necessarily amenable to spatial analysis, a wide range of physical and social characteristics can be enumerated for areas within which 'deprived' families may frequently be found :

    (i) high: immigration, overcrowding, lack of amenities; proportions of unskilled and semi-skilled workers, of large families, child deprivation and delinquency;

   (ii) low: provision of social services, play space and recreational facilities; health conditions (Holman, 1973b, 155-156).

Such a western-based assessment can be relatively easily translated into Indian conditions. However, the point of such identification, transcending cultural differences, is that it is not being claimed that socially deprived families exist only in areas with such characteristics, nor that all residents of such areas are necessarily deprived. Unfortunately, however, 'area approaches' in the administration of attempted solutions to urban social problems often appear to have assumed such misconceptions.

Thus, purely spatial approaches to urban problems at the local level must be seen, at best, as palliatives; short term means to be justified by long-term ends of coherent urban, regional or national policies of structural change which can encompass and put into perspective the root cause of spatially expressed problems and suggest possible solutions.

CHAPTER 5

Evolution of Urban Community Development in India

5.1. THE ROLE OF EXTERNAL AGENCIES

As early as 1948 Albert Mayer (of Mayer, Whittlesey and Glass, architects, engineers, town and rural planners) of New York was advising the Indian government on the pilot rural community development project at Etawah in the then United Provinces (Uttar Pradesh). But it was in the later 1950s that two significant influences from the United States were brought to bear.

In 1959 Julia Abrahamson's book 'The neighbourhood finds itself', a sociological analysis of community development in Chicago, was published. This work, at least for the government chief planner, was an inspiration (Chandrashekhara 1978), so much so that its author was invited to India, and under a programme organised by the Quaker group the American Friends Council, she helped to inaugurate, from 1964, a programme of community development in the city of Baroda (Vadodara) in Gujarat state (see 6.3. below).

Secondly, and nationally more significant, was the interest stimulated by the Ford Foundation. Correspondance between officials of the Foundation and members of the Indian government up to Nehru himself, culminated in 1956 when the Foundation provided a $22,000 grant and the part time services of a consultant (Kennedy, 1966) for a joint programme with the Indian authorities in Delhi. Initially the orientation was to be towards sports and recreation, since Ford Foundation officials envisaged a plan to combat juvenile delinquency by putting resources into deprived urban localities (Mathur, 1956). The Indians however, did not necessarily see it this way, and in 1958 a further grant of $48,000 was provided to ascertain the services of an American sociologist (Marshal Clinard) for a year's full time consultancy. During that year, the consultant and Delhi municipal Corporation, which had established a Department of Urban Community Development (under Shri Bimalamanda Chatterjee) developed the outline of

a pilot project, which the Deputy Secretary at
the Ministry of Health, at least, considered
unique, and suggested the selection of four
zones within Delhi as experimental community
development areas (Venkatasubban,1958). The
criteria for selection, it was suggested, might
include : a maximum population size of
50,000; cultural homogeneity and community of
feeling and interest within each zone should
already exist to 'constitute a manageable
group under urban conditions' ; each should be
selected to represent a different set of
problems or a different stage in community
organisation. In the latter case, one zone
might be a 'new' neighbourhood where few if any
social services and community organisation had
been established. Such a zone would enable a
pilot programme there to develop a complete
and integrated process. Another zone, on the
other hand, might represent an old established
area with welfare and community facilities
already operating. The pilot programme in this
type of zone could then develop experience
coordinating existing services, and in
integrating these with new ones.

The Ford Foundation wanted to apply some of
the philosophy and principles of the rural
community development programme (see below,
5.2.1) to the urban context, while recognising
that the administrative structure needed to be
'tooled up' to meet urban requirements. Albert
Mayer (1956) also suggested a range of
neighbourhood types within which to establish
pilot projects, and his suggestions for possible
content of those projects gave an insight into
early thinking (Table 5.1).

In 1959 the Ford Foundation finally agreed
the terms of a three year programme whereby the
Foundation would provide 100% of the first
year's financial needs, 75% of the second, and
50% for the third such that an increasing and
subsequently total role would be played by
indigenous agencies. The Foundation's grant
amounted to $155,539 for the basic task of
stimulating and establishing community and
civic consciousness, cooperation in shared
activities, identification and preparation of
local leadership and the improvement of basic
facilities (Chatterjee, 1962).

Thus the Ford Foundation backed projects in
Delhi from the 1956 pilots and subsequently in
Ahmedabad from 1960. (In the latter case a
grant of $170,000 was authorised for a 'more
typical' Indian city than Delhi, but due to
staff problems, the project was not begun until
late 1962). The government chief planner
considered the first public discussion of UCD in
India to have taken place in 1961
(Chandrashekhara, 1978). However while the
American Friends Service project in Baroda did
not get under way before 1964, municipal
initiatives had already seen attempts at
development programmes in the 1950s in Bombay
and Tatanagar, and in two refugee colonies -

Table 5.1. Possible content of pilot urban community
development schemes

A. Economic

1. Avocational : keeping poultry and kitchen gardens.
2. Vocational : improvement of existing skills and knowledge
for existing jobs, and training in new skills.

B. Social-educational

Gatherings for discussion, social activities and festivals; one
act plays; adult literacy classes.

C. Civic

1. Self-help and local action : guidance, motivation and
ultimate self-help through external loans or grants (e.g. for
tree planting, paving maintenance, cleanliness).

2. Civic contact with authorities : to overcome the restrictions
of the definite and felt ceiling to the effectiveness of the
local group.

D. Sports and games

What is the minimum space for any appreciable exercise or activity,
and can it be found, physically or financially?

Source: Mayer (1956).

- Faridabad and Nilokheri.

5.2 THE NATIONAL PROGRAMME

5.2.1 THE RURAL PROGRAMME

Before independence, the external imposition of agricultural improvement programmes coupled with attempts to raise village social conditions largely failed in their aims. The absence of a truly comprehensive attempt to improve all aspects of rural activity, and the inablity to establish a coherent understanding, amongst the people concerned, of the aims and methods of social and economic betterment, precluded the initiation of any form of community development.

In 1952, however, following a number of pilot projects, including that at Etawah, a country wide programme of rural community development was begun as part of the nation's first five-year plan. 156 so-called community development blocks were established, each comprising approximately 100 villages with total populations of 60,000 - 70,000. Guided by a consultative committee headed by the Minister of Food, Agriculture, Community Development and Cooperation, one community development officer was allotted to each block, assisted by advisors in agriculture, animal husbandry, rural industry and public health. In their turn, these officials supervised village level workers (gram sevaks) who had the task of stimulating self-help within the villages, of which they each had responsibility for between five and ten.

By the end of the first five-year plan period, it had been decided to establish a more nationally comprehensive system. 1200 so-called National Extension Service blocks were demarcated, containing a quarter of India's rural population. Eight fields were specifically declared to be within the purview of this programme : agriculture and animal husbandry, rural engineering and industry, cooperation and village government, male and female social education. Subsequent plan periods (Table 5.2) saw further significant expansion of the rural programme with a recognised distinction between intensive community development (covering half of the country by 1961) and extensive national extension (total rural coverage). In 1959 a rural nutrition programme was incorporated, with the feeding of such risk groups as pre-school children, expectant and nursing mothers. UNICEF, FAO and WHO all became involved in some measure, while for the third plan period community development per se was extended in scope to additionally cover all cooperative and development programmes and the coordination of land donation schemes.

Stated objectives of the rural development programme thus included the assistance for

family and village based agricultural and
industrial production, the provision of
educational, health and welfare programmes and
the promotion of rural housing schemes, and
later the provision of employment opportunities
and skills generally.

In such a multifaceted approach,Bhattacharya
(1972) has discerned two prime aims : to break
village isolation in a society with some
570,000 rural settlements, and to break the
isolation of different development departments,
both from each other and from the population as
a whole. This was also attempted through the
institutionalisation of village government by
what Nehru referred to as panchayati raj
(literally government by councils of five).

Inaugurated in 1958, and implemented from the
date of Gandhi's birthday in 1959 (October 2nd.)
the panchayati raj system entails three
structural levels of village government
empowered with the charge of local development
programmes (Table 5.3) through which a 'thread
of unity' (Maddick, 1970,71) is seen to run,
representing an organically linked system
enjoying popular participation with the
delegation of a wide range of functions.

Indeed at the lowest level, the village
panchayat is supplemented by meetings of all the
eligible voters of its area - the gram sabha.
With population sizes ranging from 250 to
5000 such meetings discuss programmes
implemented at village level, but such formal
powers that are held are rarely effectively
employed. Despite an alleged 99% coverage of the
rural population, problems of poor attendence,
location of meeting places, communication, local
conflict and apathy have stimulated attempts at
reform. In particular, a ceiling of 500 people
per area and more effective functions have been
suggested. Nevertheless, some success has been
achieved. In the state of Maharashtra (Jain,
1975) the 22,000 village panchayats, covering
35,000 villages, each have two seats reserved
for women and others for scheduled castes and
tribes in proportion to their numbers.
Functions are wide ranging - sanitation and
public health; public works, buildings and
communications; education, culture and social
welfare;.self- and village defence; general
administration; agriculture, forest
preservation, animal husbandry and minor
irrigation; cottage and village based
industries; and general cooperation.

Overall, however, it could be pointed out that
by the late 1960s (Maddick, 1970) the system
had achieved relatively little impact in terms
of social change. In particular it was claimed
that little impetus had been given to
questions of family planning, health and
welfare. In any case, an accurate and
comprehensive appraisal of the panchayati raj
system has been hampered by a basic absence of
adequate information and research, and by the
wide range of other agencies involved in aspects

Table 5.2 Growth and consolidation of rural development programmes.

in the early 5-year plan periods

Plan Period	Summary
First, 1951-6	Establishment of a National Extension Service and a framework for community development.
Second, 1956-61	Acceptance of community development. Especial emphasis on increasing food production. Village leader training programme inaugurated (1957). Institutionalisation of village government (panchayati raj) (1958).
Third, 1961-6	Growth and concolidation of panchayati raj. Community development training programme well established for village workers especially in the sphere of social welfare.

Source: Bhattacharyya (1972).

Table 5.3. Rural panchayati raj structure

1. Village panchayat

'Councilof five'but on average numbering 15 elected members; 219,000 councils in total. Recommended size 1000-1500 population but wide variety in relation to population density, nature of terrain etc. Guidelines of second 5-year plan : small enough to have a sense of solidarity, but not so small that personnel cannot be provided nor essential services organised.

2. Panchayati samiti

Comprising chairmen of village panchayats.covering populations of less than 80,000 (although 50,000-130,000 range). Numbering 5,400, their jurisdiction is generally coterminous with community development block areas (except in the states of Gujarat and Karnataka). Has generally come to be the principle unit of rural local government.

3. Zila parishad

Made up of panchayat samiti chairmen; their jurisdiction relates to (old revenue) districts; totalling about 330, they each encompass about a million people in some 170 villages.

Source: Maddick (1970).

of rural development, with their overlapping
activities and various aims and approaches.

5.2.2. THE URBAN PROGRAMME

While both rural and urban community
development emphasise aspects of local self
recognition, self-help, participation and
technical assistance, certain basic differences
in concept and approach inevitably exist
(Clinard, 1966). While in the former, economic
goals are specifically related to life within
the village, the latter can rarely be as
effectively comprehensive, particularly in
directly affecting a local community's economic
opportunities. Secondly, while Indian rural
life reflects long traditions, village identity
and common occupational ties, urban life allows
far greater anonymity, a greater expectation
of administrative help (albeit usually
uncoordinated), less stability, and a degree
of abstraction from traditional views and
practices. Ironically perhaps, it was the
Rural-Urban Relationship Committee Report in
1966 which recommended guidelines for a nation -
wide UCD programme. These were taken up by
central government in the same, last year, of
the third five-year plan. Fourteen pilot
projects were sponsored by the Ministry of
Health, Family Planning and Urban Development.
Initially conceived on similar lines to the
rural programme, the urban projects emphasised
community relations, self-help, participation
and governmental economic and technical
assistance. These were to have numbered twenty,
distributed amongst selected cities of over
100,000 populations, with each project
covering a population of half that size. The
projects would be functionally divided and
sub-divided. Each would contain about eight
neighbourhood (mohalla) level committees
covering about 6000 people, which in their
turn would be comprised of twelve primary units
each made up of a population of about 500.
The government made financial provision for
staffing to the extent of Rs 50,000 per project
per year, with an additional grant of Rs 15,000
for local developmental activities pursued by the
neighbourhood committee, which would be
financially matched by joint contributions from
the appropriate state government and local
authority. Costs would also be borne by central
government for training, evaluation and
research.
Having been delayed by the declaration of a
national emergency in 1962, fourteen projects
finally proceeded in 1966, and while some were
subsequently wound up, others were also later
added (Table 5.4; Fig 5.1).
This reflected the 'not very encouraging'
(Chandra & Punalekar, 1975, 7) response from the
state governments, in that project delays and
abandonment was often due to difficulties
experienced in getting clearance to undertake

Table 5.4 Urban community development projects

State	1966 project town	Project curtailed	Later additions
1. Andhra Pradesh	-	-	Hyderabad
2. Assam	-	-	Gauhati
3. Delhi	South Delhi Trans-Jamuna Colonies	-	-
4. Goa	Panjim	1968	-
5. Gujarat	Bhavnagar	-	Surat
	Rajkot	-	Jamnagar
			Baroda
6. Kerala	-	-	Quilon
7. Maharashtra	Aurangabad	-	-
8. Manipur	Imphal	-	-
9. Punjab	Ludhiana	-	-
10. Rajasthan	Ajmer	1969	-
11. Tripura	Agartala	-	-
12. Uttar Pradesh	Jhansi	1971	-
	Kanpur	-	
13. West Bengal	Salkia	1969	-
	Tollygunj	1969	

Source: Chandra & Punalekar (1975), 6.

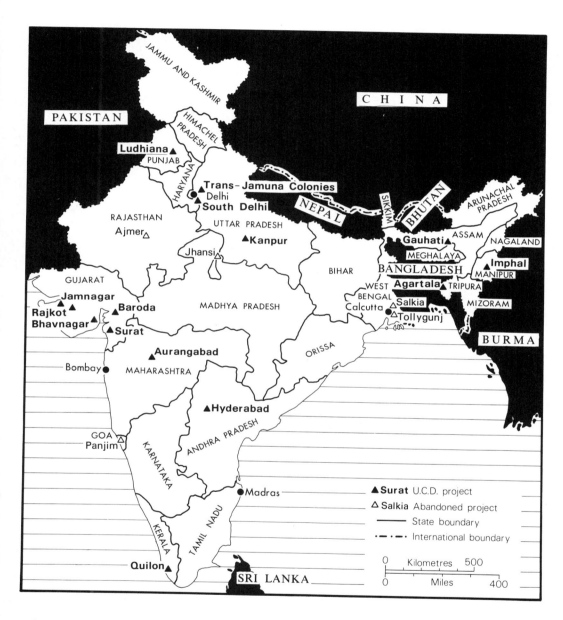

Fig. 5.1 Distribution of urban community development national programme projects.

them from that states' finance departments.

The actual selection of cities (Table 5.4) was left up to the individual states, although guidelines were set down by central government:

(i) it was recognised that there existed a desirability and an urgency to inaugurate such projects in slum areas and newly established industrial towns;

(ii) interest needed to be shown by the municipal authority and its leading officers;

(iii) the pre-existence of social agencies, voluntary organisations, universities and social institutes willing to cooperate on an experimental basis, was a necessary prerequisite;

(iv) the size and character of the towns concerned needed to be appropriate;

(v) available resources and the local authorities' own field programmes to be taken into account;

(vi) the ultimate impact the programme was likely to make needed to be anticipated.

Under these circumstances, each project was to cover a population of 50,000-60,000, and was to be divided into neighbourhood units of 6000 people, each in themselves organised with mohalla committees based upon a model constitution. Thus for each project there was recommended : a director of UCD, a project officer, four female and four male community organisers, together with voluntary workers such as craft teachers and recreation supervisors.

5.3. AIMS AND OBJECTIVES OF INDIAN URBAN COMMUNITY DEVELOPMENT

"Community development implies an induced and/or self generated process of mobilisation of physical and human resources for the purpose of promoting the welfare of all individuals of the community. No enduring community development can take place without progressively involving the community as a whole in its own welfare and without a bettering of inter-group relationships and of human relationships in general" (Delhi Municipal Corporation Department of Urban Community Development, 1959, 81).

As such, both short and long term objectives were recognised in the national UCD programme. An immediate objective was to bring about improvements in standards of living and to eliminate social conflict through the stimulation of cooperation. It was suggested that the long term aim of the programme was no

less than to evolve a new pattern of urban life.
The Ministry of Health outlined five main
objectives for the programme (Kennedy,1966):

(i) to create a sense of social coherence
on a neighbourhood basis through corporate
civic action and promoting a sense of national
integration;

(ii) to develop a sense of belonging to the
urban community through increased participation
in civic affairs, to thereby solve problems
with local initiative and cooperative self-
help;

(iii) to bring about a change in attitudes
through creating a civic consciousness and by
motivating people to improve their conditions
of life especially in terms of social and
physical environment;

(iv) to develop local initiative through
identifying and training local leaders;

(v) to ensure fuller use of available
technical and welfare services by helping the
community to locate what help can be obtained
from the municipality or other organisations,
and how it could be ascertained.

These objectives, it has been pointed out
(Chandra and Punalekar, 1975) were attempted
through five channels of activity :

(i) corporate civic action ;

(ii) the participation of people in
community affairs;

(iii) experience gained using initiative for
self-help and mutual aid;

(iv) constant motivational efforts to
stimulate the community into collective action;

(v) locating official aid sources.

The overall programme could be divided into
a number of interrelated aspects, each of
which may be given greater emphasis according
to local needs and circumstance.
Physical improvements and the development of
civic amenities entail the encouragement of
self-help through the initiative of individuals
in the community initially stimulated by
outside agencies, and through the direct use of
professional and technical assistance to support
the efforts of the people involved. As Clinard
(1966) pointed out, in any slum area this
requires the creation or consolidation of
social cohesion on a neighbourhood basis and a
reliance upon persuasion rather than
compulsion to accomplish change through people's
own efforts. Implicitly, this means that local

leadership, potential or actual, needs to be identified and supported to permeate through the local community a civic consciousness and acceptance of civic responsibility. Physical improvements such as drainage, latrines, housing repairs, water supply, paving etc. thus need to be firmly related to raising levels of consciousness regarding health, hygiene and sanitation. The introduction of facilities commensurate with levels of knowledge is essential, but when lack of experience and understanding relegate those facilities to being actual impediments to improvement, through misuse, then scarce resources are sadly wasted.

Educational, social, cultural and recreational programmes are thus of prime importance both formally and informally in helping to realise the full potential of any community development activity. Nurseries (balwadis), adult literacy classes, libraries, reading rooms and various forms of coaching must therefore take their place alongside film shows, games, sports, field outings, picnics and celebrations of all kinds.

Without raising potential economic opportunities, however, few of these palliatives would have lasting effects. Only through raising basic income levels and inculcating self respect and cooperation through gainful employment can the least ambitious improvement programmes be made realisable for impoverished slum dwellers. Thus in addition to basic educational aims, training programmes to develop basic skills in the economic sphere have been undertaken. In this way, soap, shoes, paper toys, and carpet manufacture, poultry raising, improved cooking and food preservation, and driving skills (for scooter rickshaw taxis) have been stimulated in an effort to supplement what small incomes are available to slum dwellers.

5.4. THE ROLE OF SPATIAL FACTORS

In such culturally heterogeneous urban centres as Delhi or Hyderabad (chapter 6), an understanding of culturally determined perceptions and use of residential space is a prerequisite for successful UCD. Indicated by such settlement terms as the suffixes -nagar, -pur (Hindi, Hindu) and -bad (Urdu, Muslim), urban space is often closely related to cultural considerations, and the diverse variety thereby resulting (e.g. Table 5.5). In terms of architectural design, for example, Gosh (1978) has pointed to the different space standards and space needs of cultural groups in regard to such variables as women in purdah, domestic animals, and places of worship. Thus irrespective of socio-economic status, religious and regional affiliations provide an implicit dimension of space differentiation and point to the need for the recognition of such.

In pursuing a national programme of UCD,

the Indian government established a number of
spatial criteria to be followed. UCD programmes
were to be undertaken in those areas of
greatest perceived need - slums and deprived
localities, new housing colonies within which
slum dwellers had been relocated, and mixed
hutment areas of both katcha and pucca
buildings, inhabited by low income and lower-
middle income groups. An initial aim was for
UCD to be undertaken only where local
authorities had established development plans.
But such fomalised frameworks were, to say the
least, somewhat ephemeral to the extent that
this objective was soon circumvented.

A third declared intention, that spatial
contiguity and compactness should be
prerequisite characteristics for any UCD
programme area, was again not always adhered to.
Such inconsistencies were further exacerbated
by the fact that project staff were usually
undergoing initial community development
training when their own specific urban areas
were being selected and demarcated.

As a process of transforming a problem into an
asset (Chatterjee, 1978) UCD needs to focus upon
local processes and relationships. In this
respect the interactions in space of the
physical and built environment have, superimposed
upon them, dimensions of varying social
interactions. Thus in residential areas with
narrow routeways, relationships develop most
strongly between neighbours across the path,
whereas wider and more heavily used pathways
restrict strong relationships to those between
contiguous neighbours on the same side of the
thoroughfare. Few vertical relationships would
appear to develop in multi-storey buildings of
their own accord. Thus in Gujarat state for
example, communal areas on every third floor of
high rise buildings have been established as
meeting places to generate common interests and
to accommodate such socially integrative (albeit
male dominated) public activities as hair
cutting and shaving (otherwise undertaken as a
mutual exercise out of doors). Such processes
are at the core of community development.

The role of women, within a spatial
perspective, has been seen to be particularly
crucial. In Ahmedabad it has been claimed that
women have been outstanding in their support of
UCD. Inter-communal strife (usually the preserve
of men) together with traditional male
domination tying women to their homes and
immediate neighbourhood, have restricted women
in their spatial role. Through UCD programmes
they have been a fundamental integrative
catalyst in grasping opportunities previously
denied to them, while acting out these new roles
still largely within a specific spatial context.
But it is just the local area which one of the
original Indian pioneers of UCD sees as
fundamental to Indian society :
   "...if urban communities are not broken into
   smaller units...the whole thing will explode"

Table 5.5. Spatial factors as cultural variables
in community development

Spatial prerequisite	Cultural variables
1. Compactness	Organisation of the built environment Living space Social networks and mobility patterns
2. Social homogeneity	Social differentiation - ethnic, religious/ caste, linguistic, village/regional, kin based length of residence, socio-economic
3. Homogeneity of the built environment	Morphological functions Age and status of buildings Architectural style
4. Area boundaries	Physical land use differences Psychological conceptions of barriers and differentiation

(Chatterjee, 1978).

Thus at the micro-level for example, the strategic location in UCD programmes of new taps and communal latrines is vital. As foci of community activity, particularly in spontaneous settlements and slum areas, such essential needs can be a source of tension or of integration. Thus for example, in Calcutta slums communal latrines have been located deliberately away from fringe areas (Sivaramakrishan, 1977a). Careful analysis of the location, quantity, use and maintenance of such facilities is vital for effective development programmes. Cooperative, well organised and efficient use and upkeep of such nodal points, stimulated by community workers and sustained by the dynamism of indigenous leadership can indeed transform a problem into an asset. Likewise the gradient of a drain may well be a vital factor in neighbourhood relations, determining for example, whose threshold is first to be swamped when the drain is overloaded and overflows.

Process orientation is a term much employed by Indian community workers. The process, culminating in what may be considered as successful community development, is characterised by the three cumulative concepts of : communication – within the community and between it and the development agencies; cooperation – in common activities, sharing mutual aims; and integration – of the community through the processes related to the previous two concepts.

The next chapter looks at such processes and patterns through case studies of UCD programmes in three very different cities – Delhi, Hyderabad and Baroda (Vadodara).

CHAPTER 6

Case Studies of Urban Community Development

6.1. DELHI

Take two such nebulous 'propaganda' terms as
community and development, put them together
into a frenetic social context such as urban
India, and the outcome is likely to be a
combination of heterogeneous application and
isolated success. The following three case
study cities, while representing differing
approaches to Indian UCD and emphasising the
heterogeneity of such activity, do in
themselves symbolise the differentiation
implicit not only within but between Indian
urban centres. Delhi, as India's twentieth
century capital, has expanded in an
uncontrolled fashion since independence and
partition brought to it large numbers of Hindu
and Sikh refugees from what had become Pakistan.
But as the country's administrative and
academic, of not cultural, capital, Delhi does
possess the widest range of tertiary employment
opportunities within India. Hyderabad, by
contrast, represents the nucleus of a former
Islamic ruled princely state, with a ruler
arguably the richest man in the world. Baroda,
also a former princely state capital, is
perhaps the most typically Indian city of the
three, now pursuing very much a provincial role,
having lost its capital status.

In 1830 the British under General Lake
defeated the Marathas and took the city of
Delhi — principally the walled city of
Shahjahanabad with a population of 150,000
(Table 6.1) — under their 'protection'.
Shahjahanabad had been established in 1648 as
the seventh, and last of the great Mogul cities
of the so-called New Delhi triangle (Thakore,
1962). Within the 27 feet high walls and
fourteen gates were 36 mohallas, dominated by
the citadel (Red Fort) the mighty Jama Masjid
mosque and a major commercial street (Chandni
Chauk).

Following a three month rebellion in 1857,
governmental responsibility was transferred
from the British India Company to the Crown in

January 1858. Administration of the country
was initially based in Calcutta, a process cut
short in 1911 with the official transfer of
capital functions to the planned city of New
Delhi, developed by Lutyens to the south of
Shajahanabad over a period of eighteen years.
Thus vast new venture highlighted and
magnified a process of population growth
fuelled by in-migration to which the first
railways, reaching the city in 1867, had given
impetus.

In Delhi's modern history, two major
upheavals have fundamentally modified its
demographic pattern. The first came in the
aftermath of the 1857 revolt. Shahjahanabad had
been put under marshal law, with some parts of
the city including the Royal Square, having
been destroyed. With the killing of British
soldiers, however, the inhabitants of the city
were expelled, the citadel was converted into a
barracks, and initially only Hindus were allowed
to return (Bopegamage, 1957).

More profound, however, was partition and
independence in 1947. A massive inflow of
Hindus from newly created Pakistan, with large
scale contrawise migration of Muslims
fundamentally altered the demographic structure
and cultural mosaic of many parts of north
India. Delhi was no exception to this. Indeed,
being far the largest city in north western
India, the nature of its demographic change
within a decade provides a microcosm of the
cultural transformation taking place in this
part of Asia. Whereas in 1941 the city's Hindu
and Muslim populations were reasonably balanced
at respectively 53.2% and 40.5% of the total
population , by 1951 Hindu refugees had
largely filled, to overflowing, the vacuum left
by migrating Muslims such that their
proportions had reached utter imbalance at 82.1%
and 6.6% respectively. In that year, as a
consequence, some 62% of Delhi's population
were classified as immigrants, revealing an
imbalanced sex ratio of 75.1 females per
hundred males compared with an average in the
city's satellite towns of 91.5 (Bopegamage,
1957). Such structural changes in the city's
demography were complemented by an enormous
increase in population overall : 106% in the
intercensal period 1941-51 amounting to some
740,000 persons (Table 6.1). Interestingly,
however, while New Delhi, the Civil Lines and
other suburbs were expanding in response to
population growth, the highly constricted old
core of the city became even more overcrowded.
Thus between 1931 and 1951, while Old Delhi's
population increased by some 163% (560,000),
its total area increased by just 15.8% (601.6
acres), entailing an increase in population
density from 91 to 207 persons per acre
(Bopegamage, 1957), with some mohallas in
Shahjahanabad revealing densities in excess of
a thousand persons per acre.

Partly in response to the enormous social and

Table 6.1. Delhi's population growth and density

Date	Population	Area sq.mls	Average density (persons/sq.mile)	Population growth %
1803	150,000	16.7	8,982	–
1848	160,279	16.7	9.597	6.9
1868	154,417	16.7	9,240	-3.7
1881	173,393	16.7	10,370	12.6
1891	192,579	16.7	11,518	11.1
1901	214,115	16.7	12,475	11.2
1911	237,934	16.7	13,926	11.1
1921	314,420	64.9	4,694	27.9
1931	447,442	65.5	6,834	47.0
1941	696,686	67.3	10,337	55.5
1951	1,437,134	77.5	18,556	106.6
1961	2,359,408	126.0	18,725	64.1
1971	3,620,950	174.3	20,924	53.9

Source : Census of India, 1971

financial pressures such a demographic change
exerted on the city, in 1948 the Delhi
Municipal Committee established an adult
education department, which gradually extended
its activities into the field of social
education, inaugurating such innovations as
literacy classes, reading rooms, libraries,
female craft classes and dramas.

The creation of a UCD department in 1958 with
a specific liaison programme in association
with the Ford Foundation was seen as implying a
new appraoch to emphasise initiative through
self-help complemented by limited stimulus
from public bodies. Initially therefore, an
intensive community organisation approach was
restricted to specific mohallas with a view to
developing such methods that could be
subsequently employed on a grander scale (Raj,
1972), with Ford Foundation grants (section
5.1 above) programmed for a period of $3\frac{1}{2}$ years.
The Delhi pilot project was thus designed to
encourage social integration by stimulating a
sense of civic pride and to prepare residents
for the acceptance of some municipal services by
neighbourhood development councils under local
leadership.

The lynchpin of this programme was to be the
establishment of citizens' development councils-
vikas mandals — based upon groupings of 250-
1000 families living in a compact spatial area.
These were established in no less than eleven
careful stages.

The spatial component was indeed very
important in terms of size, bounding and
psychological recognition. Wherever possible,
the names given to such areas were taken from
conspicuous streets, lanes, or from names of
locally important historical figures, in an
attempt to establish a strong psycho-spatial
association. With a marked lack of open space
or formal meeting places, however, the
organisational centres of these areas needed to
be improvised, with meetings often in alleys and
makeshift accommodation.

An evaluation and research unit employed to
establish boundaries, had a number of guidelines
to bear in mind : physical and spatial
compactness; social homogeneity; the existince
of, or the possibilities for cultivating strong
local relationships; the presence of actual or
potential common community facilities;
population size; historical identification
(Clinard, 1966). In practice, inevitably,
compromises were made between physical
structure, social composition and the presence
of social problems. The electoral roll and a
questionnaire survey were employed to
ascertain social homogeneity, while the
presence of pre-existing voluntary associations
in an area was considered a useful indicator of
spatially expressed common values. Population
size was based upon the concept of village
familiarity tempered by an areal population
based upon the notion that for intimate

community knowledge amongst residents and ease
of internal access, size should reflect the
ability of any member of the local community to
walk through an area without difficulty once or
twice daily (Chatterjee, 1978).

Reflecting the goals of such development,
each vikas mandal usually delegated activity to
five local committees to cover physical
improvements, health and sanitation, education
and literacy, recreation and culture, and
economic improvement. Each of these would be
comprised of up to three members. Clinard
(1966, 151-152) has previously detailed the
composition of the six pilot areas where vikas
mandals were established : individual areas of
very different characteristics were selected to
reflect the range of potential physical, social
and economic problems.

While vikas mandals acted as the main focus
for community development, two other tiers of
activity in Delhi were employed - zone councils
(vikas sabhas) - usually comprising 25-55
families and based upon areas reflecting social
network activity, and neighbourhood councils
(vikas parishads) made up of 1500 to 4000
families, each in its turn being part of a
political ward (mohalla) of between 25,000 and
75,000 population. Whereas vikas sabhas were
based upon small areas of local contact, and
acted as (generally) apolitical bases to be
represented by one executive member of vikas
mandal. vikas parishads' bounding did not
necessarily imply the presence of a socially
cohesive spatial area, but functioned
downwards to coordinate local activities amongst
the lower tiers, and upwards to accept
delegated service responsibilities from the
municipal corporation. In addition, vikas
sabhas, were paralleled by womens' organisations
- mahilla samitis. With the implicit male
dominance of all formal channels, mahila
samitis, each representing between fifteen and
a hundred women, could, it was argued,
articulate the specific problems, needs and
aspirations of an area's female population.
With relatively high levels of illiteracy, such
small scale and all embracing bodies are
important in transmitting communications by
word of mouth. At the level of the vikas
parishad by contrast, voluntary association
representatives, municipal councillors, zonal
health officers, sanitary inspectors and local
headmasters were all active in the council's
composition, in addition to vikas mandal
representatives. The coordination function at
this level entailed health programmes, including
immunisation and vaccination, exhibitions,
special health and cleanliness weeks. Political
and religious festivals were organised and
celebrated, while excursions, neighbourhood
competitions and summer programmes for children
were all thought of as helping to widen
aspirations and develop cooperation amongst
residents.

By the end of 1965, the six initial projects had been extended to 47 vikas mandals covering some 96,000 population with an additional 30,000 benefitting from the construction of community centres. The Corporations' UCD department had managed to undertake a survey of the aims, objectives and functions of over thirty pre-existing mohalla organisations. Their presence was an important factor in area selection, being seen as a potentially useful adjunct to the work of the department (Kennedy, 1966). Many were, however, hampered by a shortage of trained workers, and appeared to function only in times of crisis. Thus UCD training programmes were particularly aimed at such organisations' representatives.

Overall, the work undertaken within the Delhi UCD programme can be classified under several headings.

Physical improvements have ranged from levelling and repairing lanes and roads, to providing new latrines, whitewashing houses, improving drainage and water supply, and fixing house name-plates.

Health and nutrition developments have entailed vaccination and family planning programmes, talks on nutrition and child care, DDT spraying, subsidised milk distribution, and baby shows. 'Keep Delhi Clean' campaigns have encouraged donations from the business community. One project connected with World Health Week raised Rs7,500.

Education, closely related to the health and nutrition programmes, has particularly emphasised social education and literacy, with the provision and staffing of reading rooms classes and nurseries.

In the cultural and recreational field a network of community halls were established, although with such pressing housing problems, local priorities often gave non-residential buildings minimal support. Where made available, however, community halls were seen to provide an effective nucleus for community integration as well as being able to house reading rooms, libraries, handicraft classes, nursery schools and literacy programmes (but see section 7.2 point 7, below).

Bazaar projects were aimed at raising levels of environmental hygiene by stimulating bazaar associations into organising traders' groups at a city level. This was to act at the top end as a pressure group for improved conditions, while at the lower end, two community organisers would be assigned to each bazaar of about 300 shops to stimulate self-help improvements, literally on the ground.

Overall, however, it could be argued that this organisational structure was a little too formalised and inflexible, amassing a bureaucracy to soak up externally provided funds (see also section 7.2 below) :

"Although self-help paving of lanes, repair

of houses, fixing of name plates etc. were
not difficult to measure, the degree of
community feeling and inter-personal
relationship behind an artificially created
Vikas Mandal did not lend themselves easily to
a precise and scientific measurement" (Chandra
and Punalekar, 1975, 11).

While comprising part of the national UCD
programme, activity in Delhi (which had
focussed specifically on South Delhi and the
Trans-Jamuna Colonies) now appears to be a
shadow of its former self, despite rumblings
suggesting a possible phoenix-like resurgence.
The Municipal Corporation's UCD section
operates from a katra room by the Bhawa Shah
market, in the northern suburb of Kamla Nagar,
with only a skeletal staff. Perhaps this
reflects the traumas of the 1975-77 emergency
period under Mrs Gandhi and son, and in
particular the 'comprehensive' role that Delhi
Development Authority then took:

"...the Ministry of Rehabilitation (sic)
started clearance work in 1963. Shifting....
squatters through inducements, incentives and
persuasion....It is unfortunate that our
(later) experiment got enmeshed in the
extraneous factor of high politics of
emergency" (Jamohan, 1978, 17 : ex Vice-
Chairman, Delhi Development Authority).

It is in this light that specific spatial
factors relating to the above processes are
evaluated in chapter 7.

6.2. HYDERABAD

Situated in the heart of the Deccan Plateau
in what may be termed central peninsular India
(Fig. 2.1), the city (and former state) of
Hyderabad presents the historical paradox of a
Hindu populace ruled by an Islamic and
'Islamized' elite (Rao and Murthy, 1972).As an
Islamic city, Hyderabad has attracted widespread
in-migration:

"....the city was a veritable Lodestar for
young Muslims from all over India (and the
Indo-gangetic plains in particular)" (Khan,
1978b, 184).

Later, with British colonialism, the
cantonment twin-city of Secunderabad was
established (Fig 6.1). Thus of the city's 1971
population of 1.6 million (Table 6.2) some half
a million were Muslims. Since establishment of
Andhra Pradesh state, with Hyderabad as its
capital, a previous cultural dualism has been
blurred to emphasise distinctions on a
linguistic and a class basis rather than on
those of religion and caste. Moreover, three
dictinct centres have emerged (Fig 6.1)(Khan
and Gopi, 1968). In particular, South Hyderabad

Fig. 6.1 Hyderabad

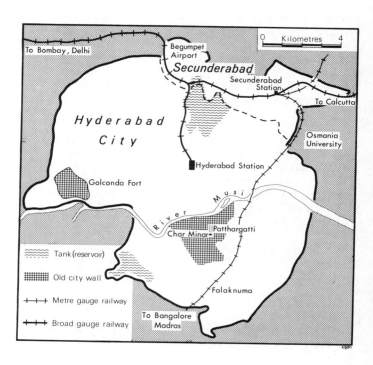

Table 6.2. Population growth of metropolitan Hyderabad

Year	Population	% growth
1881	367,417	-
1891	415,039	12.65
1901	448,466	8.29
1911	502,104	11.96
1921	405,630	-19.21
1931	447,390	10.30
1941	720,032	60.94
1951	1,026,062	42.50
1961	1,118,553	9.01
1971	1,612,276	44.14

Source : Khan (1978b), 193.

Table 6.3 Hyderabad urban agglomeration : recent growth trends

Areal Unit	Population		% growth	Density (persons/sq.ml)	
	1961	1971	1961-1971	1961	1971
Urban agglomeration	1,251,119	1,798,910	42.52	1242	1538
A. Incorporated area	1,118,553	1,612,276	44.14	1315	1895
(i) Hyderabad division	931,082	1,361,335	46.21	1342	1961
(ii) Secunderabad division	187,471	250,941	33.85	1198	1604
B. Non-incorporated area	132,566	186,634	-	845	585

Source : Khan (1978b), 191.

including the old city core, has been seen to
stagnate in contrast to growth north of the
River Musi, despite a specific Hyderabad
population growth rate of 46% between 1961 and
1971 (Table 6.3). It is here that most UCD
effort has been concentrated.

At the present time Hyderabad has two major
UCD projects operating within its boundaries.
One is part of the national programme, being
organised from the Municipal Corporation's own
UCD department (with aid from UNICEF). The other
has grown from Dutch involvement in urban and
rural social development, a strand stimulated
by the visit of Queen Juliana to Calcutta in
1966. While in the latter case we are
primarily concerned with its urban component,
the fact that it has developed from a rural
programme does lay emphasis on the catalyst
role, both conceptually and empirically, of
the rural sector in its social, economic and
political dimensions.

The first programme in Hyderabad, that of the
Municipal Corporation, also encompasses two
distinct aspects, and it is these which, in
turn, are next to be discussed.

6.2.1 HYDERABAD URBAN COMMUNITY DEVELOPMENT
PROJECT

In 1972 the city had 284 declared slum
areas, containing a total population of
272,000 (16% of the city's total). By 1978 this
figure had increased to 377 slum areas with
400,000 residents (20%).

In emphasising civic consciousness and
responsibility, an inculcation of self-help
and self-reliance are specifically seen as
replacements for criticism and condemnation in
the dominant attitudes of residents. To this
end, administrative, technical and financial
assistance are made available from the
municipal and state governments and voluntary
agencies. The role of the latter is
particularly emphasised by the former. Indeed,
the Municipal Corporation of Hyderabad claimed
(1978) to be working with some 300 voluntary
organisations in its UCD programme (a source
Delhi failed to utilise adequately), declaring
that :

"Voluntary organisations....mobilise speedy
action....can feel the priority problems of
the community at the right time....can entrust
the problem to the right person to deal with
it....can mobilise the local resources with
ease and speed....excellent media to develop
healthy and democratic leadership.....bridge
the gap between government and masses"
(Municipal Corporation of Hyderabad, n.d., 6).

Whether true or illusory, such claims do
reveal a stark contrast in approach between
this programme and the Indo-Dutch Project
(section 6.3.2 below). For in the latter,

areas were specifically chosen for their lack of
previous voluntary activity, so as to avoid a
clash of interests (Butt, 1978).
A number of distinct steps have been
recognised in the Hyderabad project as being
essential to successful UCD:

(i) identification of the felt needs of the
people;

(ii) soliciting of residents to identify
those willing to come forward and take some
part in meeting those felt needs and to thus
improve local conditions;

(iii) preparation of a formula for aid, both
financial and otherwise, and for ultimately
solving (sic) neighbourhood problems.

While the application of such an approach has
been relatively uniform within Hyderabad's UCD
areas (Table 6.5) the range of activities
undertaken has varied from area to area
according to local (perceived) needs. These are
summarised in Table 6.4.
The UCD programme was inaugurated in one of
the most heavily populated areas of the city,
with cramped, small shops and dwellings and
narrow streets. This area was south of the River
Musi and adjacent to the city's Islamic core
focussed upon the Char Minar (Fig. 6.1). This
programme was extended in 1970 encompassing two
wards in Secunderabad, and again in 1974.
Ambitiously perhaps, the whole city is now
coming under the aegis of the Municipal
Corporation's UCD department. Table 6.5
indicates the phases of growth.

6.2.2. HABITAT HYDERABAD

A part of, yet conceptually separate from the
main UCD programme in Hyderabad, is the Habitat
project, with its focus primarily on housing
conditions, with an implicit understanding that
other social and economic improvements will
accrue in the wake of an improved residential
environment.
As in the west, the 1960s and early 1970s saw
emphasis laid upon slum clearance and
replacement tenement construction, with former
slum dwellers being progressively housed in
multi-storey dwellings with subsidised rents.
In Hyderabad, some 2000 tenements were built in
this way. But as elsewhere, such a policy had
obvious social and economic drawbacks:

(i) such a capital intensive programme could
only touch the fringe of the problem being
tackled, while involving a heavy financial
outlay;

(ii) despite subsidies, the monthly rents
(Rs 26 in 1978) are usually too high for many
families who may sublet and return to slum

118

Table 6.4 Hyderabad UCD project activities

1. Free spectacles distributed - 3200.
2. Loan facilities for weaker sections (recipients) - 875.
3. Typewriting/shorthand courses (no.trained) - 720.
4. House improvements - 400.
5. Food and nutrition courses (no. trained) - 250.
6. Auto-rickshaw driving courses (no.trained) - 155.
7. Voluntary organisations initiated - 154.
8. Liaison with other agencies - 140
9. Air-conditioning and refrigeration courses (no. trained) - 114
10. Motor car driving courses (no. trained) - 80.
11. Photography courses (no. trained) - 60.
12. Fruit preservation and canning courses (no. trained) - 40.
13. Radio mechanics courses (no. trained) -37
14. Balwadies (nurseries) - 33.
15. Midday meal centres - 33
16. Computer punching and verification courses (no. trained) - 32
17. Feeding centres - 28.
18. Sewing centres - 27.
19. Self-help halls constructed - 18.
20. Rickshaw drivers' festivals - 7.
21. Eye camps - 6
22. Comprehensive medical check-ups campaigns - 4.
23. Self-help housing colonies constructed - 3.

Other activities : music centres; dance classes; cooperatives for auto rickshaw drivers; women's welfare; garment manufacturing; catering; help for the physically handicapped; study tours; youth festivals; anti-mosquito campaigns; youth leader training; children's rallies; seminars and workshops; immunisation; orientation training for social workers; public meetings and film shows; simple and inter-caste marriages; physical amenity provision.

Source : Municipal Corporation of Hyderabad (n.d.), 10-11.

Table 6.5. Phases of growth of Hyderabad's UCD programme

Starting date	Area	Resident population
1. 30/11/67	Experimental project in Ward 22, Circle 1.	48,734
2. 1/4/70	Extension to Blocks 3 & 7 of Ward 17,Circle 1, with same core staff.	31,871
3. 1/3/74	Project II : Wards 6 & 11 of Secunderabad	59,277
4. 1/3/74	Project III : Blocks 6-10 of Ward 1 in Musheerabad	69,435
5. 1/12/75	Satellite project in selected slums around the three main projects	15,566

Six additional projects with UNICEF assistance (1/4/77)

1.	Circle 4 : Ward 13 & parts of 10 & 12	79,878
2.	Circle 2 : Wards 14,15 & 21 & Blocks 3-7 of Ward 20	189,437
3.	Circle 5 : Wards 6,7,8.	117,474
4.	Circle 3 : Wards 2 & 3, & Blocks 1-5 of Ward 1.	205,702
5.	Circle 6 : Wards 4 & 5	107,253
6.	Secunderabad Division : Wards 1-5,7-10 & 12	193,507

Source : Municipal Corporation of Hyderabad (n.d.),4.

living themselves, or may occupy in extremely
overcrowded conditions; or may simply default in
rent payments;

(iii) the multi-storey flats are often built
at some distance from the original slums from
which their resident populations are being
decanted, and around which occupational and
emotional attachments have developed;

(iv) multi-storey living per se, without
direct ground level access to open space, is
also a difficult and often new context for
residents to reconcile themselves to.

With such apparent shortcomings, a slum
improvement scheme was inaugurated whereby the
environmental conditions of existing slums
could be improved through the provision of the
usual physical amenities : water supply, paved
streets, electricity, community baths and
latrines, dust bins, sewers, drains, access
roads. Eighty four slum areas with a resident
population of 147,000 were approached in this
way. But while such localities as a whole are
upgraded in this way, the fabric of the
individual dwellings remains much as before. In
particular, however, it has been found that
facilities such as community latrines soon
lapse into abuse if no one in the locality
feels responsible for them.
It is due to lessons learnt from both
approaches - redevelopment and improvement -
that Project Habitat was evolved. This 'self-
help housing programme' builds upon the local
administrative distinction between
'objectionable' and 'unobjectionable' slums. Of
Hyderabad's 377 slum areas (November 1978) 85
fall into the former category. These are
designated to be 'dealt with' (ie. ultimately
demolished) by the Housing Board since they
consist of those slums persisting on land
designated for non-residential uses; for
example, those to be affected by road widening
schemes, industrial location or the siting of
public facilities. Thus they are
'objectionable' not necessarily in the sense
that they present an impoverished and
debilitating environment, but, to employ a
British planning term, they simply represent
non-conforming land uses in relation to stated
planned functions, whether real or illusory.
The key starting point for the Habitat
programme is the fact that dwellers within the
292 'unobjectionable' slum areas, usually
located on publically owned land not
designated for non-residential uses, are given
land rights (pattas) within the city for their
rehousing. To this end, a nearby area of open
land is found for a new housing layout. Plots
of uniform size are established and type
designs are worked out. While the authorities
insist upon a uniform elevation for each
house, internal variations in relation to

family size are allowed, and there exists
scope for later vertical expansion. The total
plinth area is about fifty square metres.

Initially, however, a number of conceptual
problems need to be overcome. Firstly, there is
the perennial problem of defining what a slum
is. When asked, Hyderabad's UCD department will
claim to use the standard United Nations
definition. When pressed further, they agree
that such a definition is very generalised and
of course culturally relative. Thus in fact,
while taking such a definition into account, in
any given situation the UCD director himself
makes the final classificatory decision after
both his department's survey unit has inspected
an area, and the health department has reported
upon it (Rao, 1978). So how restricted or
'generous' is the UCD department in its
allocation of the term 'slum' to residential
areas in relation to its own limited resources
for ameliorating such areas? Not suprisingly,
the definition is restricted, but with social
consequences the reverse of which might have
been expected in western society. Because of
the likelihood that once an area is designated
as a slum, resources will flow, many low
socio-economic group residents, apparently
devoid of any sense of stigma, positively
demand that their area be designated as a slum
so as to be able to share resources thereby
allocated. Thus boundary disputes and
allocation problems are likely to follow,
although the writer was assured by Hyderabad
officials that there tended to be only "10%
disagreement" with residents regarding slum
definitions (Rao, 1978). For example, in a
heterogeneous area being improved rather than
redeveloped, 60% of dwellings might be
designated as slums but the remaining 40% not
so designated might at the same time be
inextricably part of the same area. In such
cases the major infrastructural elements of
improvement - water supplies, sewage control,
paving etc. - are introduced for the whole area,
but individual help - regarding internal house
improvements, social and economic opportunities
etc. - is only offered to the residents of the
designated 60%

In deciding whether to improve an area or to
apply Project Habitat principles, the nature of
the slum population is of paramount importance.
As we have already seen, the heterogeneous,
multiplex and cross-cutting nature of Indian
urban social life makes model building and
generalisation difficult . Religion, caste,
sex, employment, origin, language, age all play
an important role in the mosaic of urban
socio-spatial patterns. But in relation to slum
renewal, the dichotomy between long term
residents and migrants is especially important.
The former, having developed over years
emotional, social, cultural and economic
attachments to their place of residence, however
impoverished and decrepit, are usually loath to

see it demolished to be rehoused. Thus within the constraints of resource availability, improvement rather than reconstruction is the policy that Hyderabad's UCD department attempts to pursue in areas of long term residence. In migrant areas by contrast, where short term residence is buttressed by outside allegiances, little attachment is felt for the existing fabric, and redevelopment is often the preferred course of both resident and official.

Returning to the Habitat programme, its main features can be summarised as incorporating three areas of operation :

1. House building : the self-help concept is developed to the extent that of the average Rs 5,200 cost of each new house, the Municipal Corporation of Hyderabad helps to ascertain loans of Rs 4,000 per family, at interest rates of 4%, repayable monthly over ten years, from the major banks (State Bank of India, Bank of Baroda, State Bank of Hyderabad, Allahabad Bank etc). Aid is also sought from philanthropic organisations such as Rotarians, Lions and Jaycees. Thus for example, in East Lions Nagar 130 families each received Rs 500 from the Lions Club of Hyderabad East, leaving an outstanding Rs 700 for each family to find by way of money, labour, or material towards construction. Additionally, Hyderabad's engineering department supervises the actual construction of the houses, which are based upon approved plans of design and layout, and to this end is able to ascertain bulk purchases at reduced rates in such commodities as cement. However,

"there is need for a slightly liberal and practical approach on the part of town planners for preparing a layout based not on the rigid code of building bye-laws but on practical compromises" (Municipal Corporation of Hyderabad, 1978,3).

2. Construction of major infrastructural needs : access roads, drains, lights, water, latrines, dust bins, is undertaken by the Municipal Corporation with the aid of grants from the Andhra Pradesh state government.

3. Formation and implementation of socio-economic programmes (Table 6.4) are pursued to bring about behavioural changes in the existing living and working patterns of slum dwellers and improve their quality of life to "eliminate the 'mental slum' " (Rao, 1978). For this purpose, area based community development workers – basti sahayaks – are attached to and live in individual schemes to stimulate motivation and acceptance amongst the slum families. They work under divisional UCD officers – 'community organisers' – whose role it is to liaise between the Municipal Corporation, the lending banks and voluntary

agencies, and to oversee the socio-economic
progress of the Habitat schemes within their
division.

The proposal to encompass 10,000
residential units under the project had seen
6691 units within 64 areas covered by September
1978, in the stages as outlined in Table 6.6.

One project area in the final stages of
construction when visited (November 1978) was
that of Naiknagar, situated to the south of the
city's southern centre in the Falaknuma
district (Fig. 6.1). Here, 350 families were
being rehoused from straw and mud huts settled
when the area was situated on the city's
periphery. As the final 100 houses were being
built, with groups of ten families working on
10 houses at a time, the finishing touches were
also being put to the area's community hall.This
modest structure, located next to a stagnant
pond designated for draining, was constructed
by the residents for marriages and festivals,
and although somewhat spartan, contained a
television (50% of whose cost was contributed by
the Hyderabad authority) for the use of all
residents. Six communal water taps were
considered adequate for the 350 families, and
electricity was "coming soon". Certainly the
pragmatism earlier suggested in building style
was reflected in the earliest houses of the
scheme being fronted by self-built patio/
kitchens, often surrounded by lime and mango
trees, with decreasing evidence of such
laissez faire building activity with increasing
newness of the houses, as one passed down the
grid planned, whitewashed rows. Such flexibility
is to be welcomed, but one wonders how, with
increasing aspirations stimulated by an
improved environment, the life style of this
particular group will change. For the Naiks, an
'unscheduled tribe', speaking a langauage –
Lumbara – without a written script, migrated
from the Rajastan forests in the noth west of
the country over 200 years ago, settling
particularly in Hyderabad (some 50,000) and
Pune. The women still wear traditional dress, a
physically inhibiting combination of tight arm
bands from wrist to upper arm, long ankle length
multicoloured garments tight at the waist and
encumbered with all manner of appendages for
every day use, a similarly multi-hued head
covering, and enormous chandelier like earrings
dripping down to chin level. Predominantly
employed in manual labour, particularly
construction work, the sight of a row of a
dozen or more similarly clad women, and their
children, squatting, chipping away at an old
road surface with the barest of implements,
leaves a lasting impression.

Under the UCD programme, each woman can earn
four or five rupees in the sewing centre
cooperatives, while their children are provided
with bread and basic nutrional supplies such as
eggs, by the Corporation through its nursery
school programme. The economic viability

Table 6.6 Project Habitat Hyderabad : stages of development as at 1.9.1978

Stage	Units	Slum Areas	Remarks
1. Motivation	2254	26	Residents having been motivated to join the cheme.
2. Processing	1267	18	Loan application being processed by the lending banks.
3. Construction	3170	20	Loans forthcoming from banks and construction under way or about to commence.
	(1077 completed)		
Totals	6691	64	

Source : Municipal Corporation of Hyderabad (1978),7.

particularly of the women's cooperatives, has however, been questioned. Whereas programmes from pedal to auto-rickshaw driving can increase a person's income by 300% once the initial capital outlay (with bank loan asistance) has been made, it has been argued that by producing goods usually already well supplied from other sources, the female cooperatives are often not economically viable. In particular, despite capital investment in sewing and embroidery machines, the cooperatives are relatively isolated in relation to the market, and with poor marketing facilities (no doubt at least partially the result of erratic production) cannot compete with established suppliers who have their own contacts and named labels.

6.2.3 THE INDO-DUTCH PROJECT FOR CHILD WELFARE

In 1966 Queen Juliana of the Netherlands passed through Calcutta and was appalled by what she saw. Organising a number of paediatricians from the World Health Organisation, a development plan for the foundation of Indian child welfare projects was established. With similar projects in Tanzania and Peru, the Dutch sought not to approach the problem in a semi-imperialistic way by inappropriately sending money and/or experts on masse, but by stimulating indigeneous efforts on a non-charitable basis, to improve their own quality of life, and in particular for that of their children.

In 1970 a plan designated to last eight to ten years was inaugurated in the rural hinterland of Hyderabad to stimulate and integrate health, education and nutrition programmes. Three prerequisites were laid down for such an area : that it should be relatively close to the city for access; that it experienced a low socio-economic status (by Indian standards) and was genuinely in need; and that no other organisations, voluntary or statutory, were working in the area, to avoid a potential clash of interests. Emphasising participation - in money, grain or services - rather than charity, the rural programme (in Chevala block, 100,000 population) undertook a conscious effort to actively involve the population. Village women, for example, were encouraged to produce standardised 'protein packets', sold by the project to residents thereby raising nutrition standards and allowing an improvement in female economic status (at a profit of five paise per packet). Thus within three years the project could claim to have overcome malnutrition amongst 7,000 children (Butt, 1978). By emphasising child care and child survival, a family planning programme was established whereby parents were shown that birth rates could be reduced by ensuring that all their children survived, thus both reducing infant mortality and raising mothers'

health chances by slowing down the succession
of births.

Undertaking such policies largely through
locally trained indigeneous workers presented
manifold problems. Prejudice against paramedics,
both from residents and doctors' associations
often reflected the lack of awareness of a
preventive role such people could play, rather
than that of simply distributing drugs as an
ameliorative palliative. In a new programme
begun in 1976, for example, whereby a male and
a. female worker were assigned to population
groups of 5,000, one year's supply of drugs
was being used up in four months. As a
consequence, in February 1978 more emphasis
was put upon the role of the village woman -
gramsvasthika - who, with schooling up to
fifth grade, would receive a 40 days crash
course of training to then work for two hours a
day assisting and providing information on
pregnancy, lactation and malnutrition, but
specifically not dispensing drugs. In
attempting to overcome prejudice against female
employment 135 village women were trained during
the first year of this programme.

Building upon knowledge gained from these
health policies and their associated educational
and economic programmes, an Indo-Dutch urban
project was inaugurated in 1977. It
incorporated two areas of South Hyderabad -
five blocks within ward 19 and blocks I and II
of ward 20 - providing a combined population of
55,000. This project was particularly innovative,
however, in that careful preparation and
groundwork was firstly laid. A detailed house
to house survey was undertaken by eight workers
(initially graduates who were found not to be
effective and were replaced by voluntary
workers). Inquiries of residents were made into
what changes and improvements were considered
locally desirable, and into the potential level
of participation in any local projects pursued.
The positive response to this survey is set
out in Table 6.7 below.

Not surprisingly, however, once the project
was begun, the actual level of response and
participation fell below such figures.
Entailing a cost of two rupees per month for
the health plan, many families found
themselves unable to afford participation. For
every thousand families the plan had made
provision for one creche, two balwadis
(nurseries), one mohilla mandal (women's club)
a youth club, library, community hall and
the health plan. Of these, the latter in
particular appeared to be misinterpreted - it
lacked doctors, so that residents had no
confidence in the paramedical personnel. It
was essentially preventative with a minimal
dispensing of pills - this again did not meet
residents' expectations. Nevertheless, after a
somewhat mixed reception, the programme had
gathered momentum in its second year of
operation such that, for example, while

Table 6.7 Positive responses to potential participation by
residents in Hyderabad survey areas

Plan	% positive response
1. Balwadi	68.7
2. Health improvement	57.5
3. Creche facilities	46.1
4. Mohilla mandal	41.2
5. Youth club	10.7

Source : Butt, 1978.

resident contributions to the project from blocks I and II in ward 20 only amounted to 31.0% and 38.7% respectively of the 1977 cost of food and salaries, for the first six months of 1978 the contributions had risen to 40.9% and 54.5%

The two approaches taken in Hyderabad thus present both interesting parallels and contrasts. The constraints met in attempting to undertake both approaches are ones familiar to most projects elsewhere, and are thus incorporated into the analytical model in chapter 7. Finally, this chapter looks at a further approach taken to UCD, in Baroda city.

6.3. BARODA (VADODARA)

Within a rich rural hinterland, Baroda, until independence, flourished as the capital of an enlightened princely state, with an important university. Now the third city within Gujarat state (Fig. 5.1) and twenty-second largest in India, Baroda had a 1971 population of 467,487, which represented no less than a 50.94% increase over its 1961 total of 298,398. Even so, in that decade, it had been overhauled by the even more spectacular growth of Surat (site of the first English factory in India) from 288,026 to 493,001 (55.27%).

After having examined some 110 Indian cities, the American Friends Service Committee and UNICEF chose Baroda as the setting for a UCD initiative. In conjunction with three relevant tiers of government - central government, Gujarat state government and the Baroda Municipal Corporation - a pilot project was begun in 1964 with an aim of raising levels of living and expectations in slum areas largely through stimulated self-help. With approximately 12% of the city's population living in administrately defined slum areas - 50,000 people and 3,560 enumerated animals (Khatu, 1978b) - Baroda's housing problem is not on a scale comparable with either Delhi or Hyderabad.

Initially four neighbourhoods were selected, each being assigned one female and one male community organiser. A number of specific criteria, both spatial and aspatial, were laid down for the demarcation of such areas. Each must have a recognisably distinct name, coterminous with the area. The size should be such to incorporate between 500 and 800 families, considered to be a workable unit. Each would be of a different social composition, but embodying overall internal homogeneity, while in each case residents would fall into the category of 'economically weaker' groups (see Appendix I). To avoid potential problems of political fragmentation or conflict, each chosen area was to be demarcated within the confines of ward boundaries with no overlap between wards. In a similar philosophical approach to that taken by

the Indo-Dutch Project in Hyderabad, areas were
only finally chosen if no previous
organisations had been operating there on a
full time basis, to avoid a duplication and
waste of resources and effort. Certainly most
pre-existing formal voluntary associations in
Baroda tend to operate more at the city level
rather than on a neighbourhood basis. Only
youth clubs, mohilla mandals, and the like
performed a function specifically at the local
level, and here often only spasmodically,
being activated in response to specific
occasions such as festivals and marriages, with
relative inactivity for much of the year.
Additionally, such organisations tended to be
sexually segregated.

In November 1969 this inaugural project was
officially handed over to the Baroda Citizens
Council, a voluntary group of up to 27 members
composed of nominees of Baroda Municipal
Council, Baroda University, Gujarat state
government, local industrialists, trade
unionists and social workers. Aiming to
coordinate and cooperate with local, voluntary
and governmental agencies, the Citizens
Council saw its prime objective as encouraging
the development of responsible citizenship to
create more effective participation. In this
respect, its terms of reference included the
sponsoring and managing of development projects;
the coordination of heighbourhood based
voluntary agencies (where they existed); the
recommendation of further courses of action to
official and non-official bodies; the
encouragement of the search for city-wide
solutions to problems unable to be solved at
the neighbourhood level; if necessary, the
stimulation of new agencies; the undertaking of
research and other scientific work (Baroda
Citizens Council, 1974).

The common approach of discerning local
leaders to act as the catalyst for action was
adopted. In each area residents were asked to
give the names of those whom they considered to
be the local leader and to whom they would go
for advice or help. Individual interests and
attempts at representing consensus views were
given voice at local meetings to emphasise to
residents that personal problems were shared
problems and for the collective betterment
local people needed to come together in
cooperative action. Gaining residents'
confidence was a major hurdle to be negotiated.

As in Delhi and Hyderabad, a wide range of
social, economic, cultural and physical
improvements have been attempted with residents'
assistance. In particular, with tradition acting
against female emancipation (eg. it is very
difficult of not impossible, for women to open
their own bank accounts), women's groups have
been seen to be an important instrument in
raising local levels of aspiration. Thus
savings groups were formed specifically to
allow women to accrue their own income through

such joint activities as sewing and selling
vegetables.

One point of emphasis has been the
requirement for Citizens Council workers to
withdraw from specific neighbourhoods once a
programme has been firmly established, with
local residents taking full responsibility for
such activities as nurseries, skill training,
latrine maintenance and social events. This
philosophy has also been imparted into other
philanthropical groups such as the Rotarians
and Lions, in an effort to fully emphasise the
role of citizen participation in the
improvement of Indian society even in the
humblest of surroundings.

One particular programme is worthy of further
scrutiny, that of the Council's employment
referral service. Theoretically, a nationwide
system of employment exchanges is available
free of charge, but because of widespread
illiteracy, large numbers of particularly
unskilled workers are apparently unaware of the
service. Moreover, vacancies notified through
employment exchanges are those of a permanent
or semi-permanent nature, usually requiring
some educational qualifications. Thus even
aware of such opportunities, the unemployed of
many depressed areas are not qualified for the
vacancies. But even if they were qualified, the
exchanges have accumulated such long lists of
registered unemployed that any new registration
would be of no use to persons who did not have
something to fall back on for several years. On
the other hand, temporary openings often occur,
about which the employment exchanges are rarely
notified, and while not providing the relative
security of a more permanent job, such
employment provides experience, develops
contacts with employers and thus increases
chances of further employment.

With this in mind, the Citizens Council
conducted a survey during 1970-1 to assess the
manpower requirements of Baroda's manifold
industries. Some 3,000 openings were discovered,
of which unskilled workers could account for a
sizeable proportion. It was also found,
however, that some employers were only willing
to pay wages actually lower than the level set
down by minimum wage laws.

"The market conditions were such that cheap
unskilled labour was available from the near
rural areas, where agricultural wages were far
lower. It was imprudent to deal with the
question in a legalistic manner with factory
owners. They would not like to disturb their
entire wage structure to oblige the Council"
(Khatu, 1977,9).

Despite such an acquiescent attitude,
employers generally did raise wage levels once
Council referrees had established their worth
and reliability. Thus in the first five years of
such a policy 441 persons had been placed in

employment by the programme.

Table 6.8 reveals the various preferences of persons placed according to educational background for the period 1970-1973.

Such aspirations were considered not to be unrealistic in all but about 3% of cases, generally those wishing to become clerks or technicians who were without an adequate level of education. By comparison, Table 6.9 reveals the actual selection rate for candidates for the years 1972 and 1973.

The lack of skills made apparent by such analyses further buttressed the development of skill training referral schemes. The number of places available at any one time, both under Council auspices and referrals, is shown in Table 6.10.

Three different cities revealing a far from standardised approach to UCD have thus been examined. Delhi, with perhaps least tangible success appeared to overemphasise the hierarchical nature of its organisational structure to the point of bureaucratic obscurantism.

Sparse resources, both in finance and manpower, once the Ford Foundation had withdrawn, the traumas of the emergency (1975-77) and the city's ever increasing growth rate all perhaps draw attention away from the localised spatial constraints examined in the next chapter. It has been suggested that Delhi's approach was too overtly supportive of the status quo (de Souza, 1978) and where it was not, opposition from local councillors fearing loss of power reduced its effectiveness (Datta, 1978). The role of such mechanisms as protection rackets, bribery and corruption, particularly in relation to spontaneous settlements, is also very difficult to assess. Certainly high density slums represent

"a high yielding variety of votes " (Chatterjee, 1978).

since the one possession the Indian poor do hold in 'the world's largest democracy' is the right to cast their ballot in favour of whoever can promise them most.

Table 6.8 Work level preferences of candidates according to educational
background (for the period 1970-1973)

Preferences	Illit.	<7yrs	Non-matric	Matric-ulates	Graduates & above	Total	%
1. Professional & technical	0	3	1	11	7	22	8.2
2. Clerical	3	0	4	44	12	63	23.4
3. Sales workers	0	1	1	1	1	4	1.5
4. Transport & communications	2	4	5	2	0	13	4.8
5. Craftsmen & production process workers	7	15	17		0	48	17.8
6. Services, sports & recreation	0	0	0	1	0	0	0.4
7. Unskilled	12	47	28	5	0	92	34.2
Not available	1	7	7	7	7	26	9.7
Totals	25	77	63	77	27	269	
%	9.3	28.6	23.4		10.0		100.0

Educational Background

Table 6.9 Job referrals, selection and take up, 1972-3

Occupation	Referred	Selected	Withdrew	Joined	As % of referrals	Av.monthly pay in Rs
1. Industrial crafts workers	60	17	6	11	18.3	124
2. Drivers	9	2	0	2	22.2	125
3. Clerks, Typists, time keepers	31	7	0	7	22.6	191
4. Sales workers	19	5	0	5	26.1	175
5. Unskilled office workers	48	16	4	12	25.0	108
6. Unskilled production process workers	87	41	5	36	41.4	82
7. Others	27	10	1	9	33.3	116
Not available	64	24	7	17	26.6	80
Totals	345	122	23	99	28.7	102

Source :Khatu (1977), 11.

Table 6.10 Places in training and training referral schemes

Field	No.	%
A. Under Council Auspices		
1. Stitching	59	
2. Motor driving	23	
3. Carton pasting	71	
4. Food craft	20	
5. Plumbing	21	
6. Spinning	53	
7. Carpentry	18	
8. Salesmanship	10	
	275	76.0
B. Referrals		
1. Typing	47	
2. Others (including candle making, soap making, welding)	40	
	87	24.0
Totals	362	100.0

Source : Khatu (1977), 17.

CHAPTER 7

Evaluation of Urban Community Development Policy in India

7.1. CONCEPTUAL FRAMEWORKS FOR SPATIAL ANALYSIS

Before evaluating Indian UCD policy within a spatial perspective, a brief discussion of alternative conceptual frameworks is needed.

A systems framework, firstly, presents its components in a formalised way as dynamic and interrelated grouped activities and objects. It has been seen as useful in defining and handling problems (although much more has often been claimed, eg. Bertalanffy, 1951,1967), and, for example, can point to the interactional nature of administrative and political behaviour, and of that behaviour with the environment. Thus systems approaches can emphasise what is sometimes regarded as the organic nature of cities, and the roles of each component part of that organism in making up the whole.

Systems applications in planning (e.g. McLoughlin, 1969: Chadwick, 1966, 1971) have been widely criticised however, criticism which is also appropriate in assessing the validity of such a framework for evaluating UCD policy. It would concentrate heavily upon physical processes, often with the false assumption that all space is absolute. Its employment would also represent an implicit acceptance of consensus attitudes, lacking scope for the accommodation of conflict theory. While simplifying complex problems, the descriptive abstraction of a system from its social context tends to buttress the attitude held by many bureaucrats, not least in India, that any subject is susceptable to numerate explanation and quantitative representation. Indeed, systems approaches often entail a 'bamboozle' function (Bailey, 1975, 68) whereby the nature of information presented to the public confuses and draws a veil of mystique around the assumptions and aims of that information.

Finally, confronted with the complexity of urban areas, it is usually impossible to actually define system boundaries, such that

the resultant open systems add little
conceptual value to any analysis.

One of the major arguments against the use of
systemic models is their implicit assumption of a
consensual society. By contrast, conflict
approaches view conflict as a basis of social
change, not least in processes of
participation and resource allocation. Marxian
in inspiration, the notion of class polarisation
and inherent conflict in non-socialist society,
however, denies 'liberal' solutions to social
problems, and refuses to acknowledge that
social conflict could represent an adjusting
and ultimately stabilising feature of society.
According to this 'true' conflict approach
(Bailey, 1975), conflict is a necessary pre-
condition of radical social change and is
implicitly located within the social structure
rather than within individual personality. By
contrast, the functionalist viewpoint (eg.
Coser, 1956), views conflict as an ultimate
function of order, and has been applied by
anthropologists to a wide range of societies.

By emphasising consensus and conflict as
polar opposites, conflict approaches tend to
ignore the modifying constraints which
ultimately produce the infinite subtle
variations of human interaction. A 'realistic'
model is thus sought to accommodate the wide
range of factors relating to decision making
and resource distribution processes in UCD
policy. A 'constraint' framework whereby both
consensus and conflict are modified through
various constraint dimensions, is suggested
(a more sophisticated model of which may be
found in Hall, 1978).

This model will be applied in a somewhat
simplified form (Fig 7.1) to spatial aspects of
UCD policy in India to focus upon the
constraints, both inherent and induced, within
contemporary Indian urban society that are
exerted upon such policy. An evaluation of such
constraints upon past and present activity will
be complemented by an assessment of the
geographical implications for public policy.

7.2. EVALUATION THROUGH A CONSTRAINT FRAMEWORK

From such external influences as outlined
earlier (eg. section 5.1) the government's
chief planner (Chandrashekhara, 1978) recognised
the need, in urban India, of reviving a
spatially based, locally derived community
spirit to parallel that supposedly found in the
Indian village. The major difference being, of
course, that new urban populations are in large
measure rural in-migrants from a wide range of
regional, linguistic, religious/caste
backgrounds. Certainly, while agglomeration of
like groups does take place, the overall
heterogeneity of urban cultural life does not
necessarily ameliorate the vast physical,
social and economic problems besetting
unplanned urban growth. As has been emphasised,

with such fundamental differences as scale,
structure, causes and consequences, Indian
urbanisation would appear to have little in
common with its North American (or indeed
Western European) counterpart, apart from
operating within an essentially non-communist
social, economic and political environment.
What then of a process designed to 'improve'
certain facets of such an environmental being
transmitted from one culture to another? One
remark made to the author repeatedly by Indian
field analysts, was that the concept of 'urban
community' was not Indian (see section 4.1
above). While spatial proximity in a village
context may sustain and buttress shared
interests and aspirations, urban spatial
proximity signifies little in itself.

Thus Indian UCD workers have often started
with a concept which, if not exactly alien,
may have been extremely difficult to be
comprehended by language, caste and kin
orientated slum dwellers. That is not to
equate slum dwelling and illiteracy with low
levels of comprehension generally. Indeed, in
many sectors of Indian urban life the inability
to read or write is often more than compensated
for by a wide range of articulatory abilities,
perception and intuition.

In the foreward to an evaluation of seven UCD
projects carried out in the early 1970's it was
claimed that

"despite various handicaps and limitations,
low inputs and half hearted attention and
support given to the programme of urban
community development, the projects have been
able to make notable headway by sensitizing
people to their needs and problems, bringing
their aspirations and discontents to surface,
arousing their sense of responsibility and
surcharging their motivation to improve their
conditions of living through self-help and
assistance from various government departments
and voluntary agents " (Chatterjee, 1975, iii-
iv).

Yet those handicaps and limitations, low
inputs and half hearted attention and support
have been sufficient to seriously reduce the
overall effectiveness of Indian UCD in the face
of mounting social, economic and physical
problems in India's towns and cities. Many of
these constraints are, of course, aspatial,
although it could be argued that the very
spatial nature of UCD is in itself a prime
constraint by virtue of the need to demarcate
specific areas of operation, areas which, in
themselves, may not represent any meaningful
psychological abstraction to residents in terms
of social, physical or economic goals.

The constraint model (Fig. 7.1) is a vehicle
to evaluate, within a spatial perspective, UCD
processes enacted in India, examining the
filtering systems which transform what appear

138

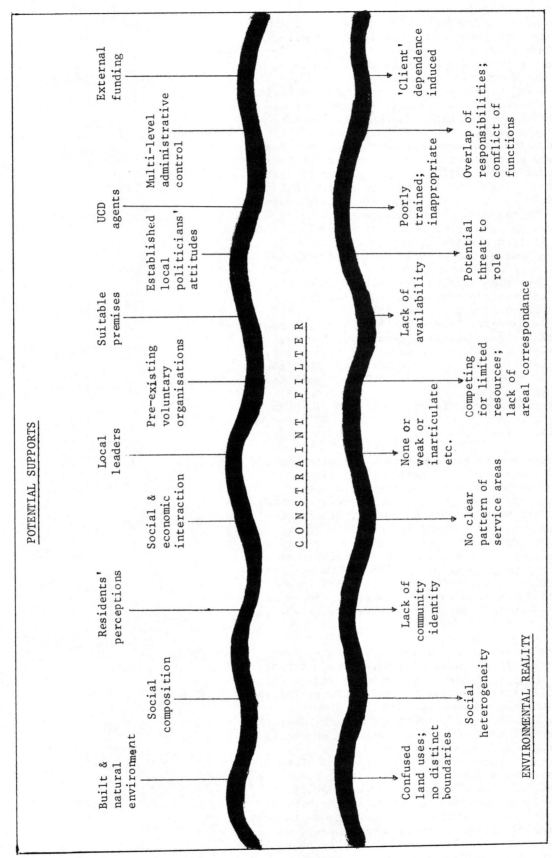

Fig. 7.1 Urban community development constraint model

to be potential supports for such processes
into somewhat less than bountiful aspects of
environmental reality. This model is simply
abstracting a range of the most significant
components contributing to UCD processes and is
postulating, in every case, a constraint filter
to render them less effective for UCD purposes.
It is the intention for the remainder of this
chapter to exemplify these constraints, and to
discuss their geographical implications for
public policy in India (section 7.3) before
finally summarising the overall conclusions
(7.4).

The strands of structural constraints
impinging upon UCD processes may be viewed
vertically, in terms of the filtering of ideas
and action between residents, UCD workers,
municipal and state bureaucracies; or
horizontally in respect of the divergent social
networks, employment structures, physical
fabric, information flows and migration patterns
within and between different parts of the city.
By focussing upon a specifically spatially
based constraint framework, the model under
discussion is viewing constraints - vertical,
horizontal, institutional and indigenous - in
terms of their effects, either actual or
perceived, upon specific spatial contexts. That
is not to say, however, that problems purely
derive from, or can be solved by specific
reference to individual areas. Indeed, it has
previously been shown (section 4.4. above) that
area based local policies often fail to
recognise the root cause of apparently localised
problems as lying within the wider social,
economic and political environment (eg. see
Hamnett, 1979). The spatial model employed
therefore implicitly accepts the aspatial
nature and origins of many problems and
attempted solutions to them. What it does throw
light upon is the perception of those problems
and attempted solutions in relation to
specific milieux of Indian urban life.

In the UCD constraint model (Fig. 7.1) eleven
components are enumerated. These may be
classified into three groups : 'internal'
constraints (nos. 1-7) which can be seen to
impinge upon UCD processes from within any
given spatial context, although their origins
may not necessarily reside in that context;
'external' constraints (10-11), those enacted
outside of such a territorial unit; and
'transcendant' constraints, interacting between
internal and external environments to exert
further filtering agents upon UCD policies
(8-9). These will now be discussed in turn.

A. 'INTERNAL' CONSTRAINTS

1. THE BUILT AND NATURAL ENVIRONMENT

Underlying most approaches to UCD has been
the basic premise that policies need to be
directed at specific 'neighbourhoods' within
the urban fabric, and that for the enaction of

such a policy physical delimitation needs to
take place, as exemplified by the criteria laid
down in Baroda (Section 6.3), aside from the
problems of the relationship between
'community', and spatial contiguity, and the
efficacy of 'community' as a relevant concept at
all within the Indian urban context (point 3
below), the role of the built and natural
environment is fundamental in both directly
and indirectly constraining UCD policy
applications. Areas need to be bounded, and the
absence of 'natural' boundaries in the urban
fabric presents fundamental logistical problems.
Not only do area based policies need boundaries
of a physical nature, whether they be
thoroughfares, notable buildings, a river,
railway, sloping ground, or a change of land
use. They must also be recognised to be
boundaries by the residents living within and
outside them. Often, in the Indian context,
this is so only if the physical component is
buttressing and spatially expressing some
degree of socio-cultural division.

Within the present context little research
has been undertaken into such cultural –
morphological relationships on a microscale.
Certainly the experience of the present writer
would suggest that in contexts of relative
cultural homogeneity, land uses such as open
space, public buildings and demolition sites
(all easy prey in India to the encroachment of
spontaneous settlements) do not contribute to
strongly held psychological boundaries, but are
more likely to provide relatively indeterminate
'frontiers' (Hall, 1979) between locally
accepted community areas.

Area size, compactness and contiguity are
fundamental variables in UCD application. They
are all, however, subject to the disposition of
land uses, which may well confound
sophisticated quantitative analyses employed to
evolve desired configurations. (eg. Blair and
Biss's (1967) method for measuring shape). One
of the pilot vikas mandal areas in Delhi for
example, consisted of 265 slum families
within an area which extended along two sides
of a long, fairly wide lane, and around three
smaller lanes leading off, the long lane once
having been connected to the old city rampart
(Clinard, 1966, 152).

2. SOCIAL COMPOSITION

Population size and density are further
basic parameters for areal delimitation. They
are likely to be interdependent in that Indian
urban population densities are generally much
higher than their western counterparts, with
both gross and net figures presenting
similarities. Thus the population size within
any given 'neighbourhood' is likely to be much
larger than that, for example, suggested for an
English neighbourhood council (Department of
the Environment, 1974) or a Scottish community

council (Scottish Development Department,1974). Such densities in inner urban areas are still increasing (eg. Delhi's Shahjahanabad), and it could well be argued that within such a dynamic demographic situation, an area with today's appropriate population size could tomorrow be overflowing with a level of residents inappropriate for today's declared policies.

Further, while population size has often been a major criterion (cf. Delhi, section 6.1 and Baroda 6.3) the qualitative characteristics of that population - particularly age and sex distribution - have rarely been considered or examined in detail. Perhaps more importantly, the cultural heterogeneity of Indian urban populations in terms of regional and linguistic affiliations, kinship and religious/caste networks, has often confounded attempts to distinguish and delimit 'homogeneous populations'. Wiebe (1977), for example, has pointed to the way in which social and cultural patterns tie slum dwellers intimately to patterns of their well-to-do neighbours. Thus in the Delhi pilot project a cross-section of six areas was initially focussed upon - some heterogeneous, others 'homogeneous' - in a not necessarily successful attempt to reflect differing cultural needs within the urban fabric.

Social differentiation in terms of income levels, and implicitly, levels of expectation, has also been seen to impose constraints on the effectiveness of UCD policy. Chatterjee (1978) has suggested that the poorer the residents, the more disposed they appear to be to share in self-help and cooperation schemes. From this notion, however, one can hypothesise a level of living, however variable, above which residents will lose the desire for sharing, since they feel they have achieved something which now needs protecting from the depredations of others. If it is realistic to postulate such a socio-economic threshold point, as revealed in parts of Delhi, then a strong argument can be put forward for UCD inputs being phased out once a resident population has generally reached such a level, otherwise the law of diminishing returns is likely to set in.

A second 'inverse relationship' could be established in terms of housing tenure. It has been argued (Chandrashekhara, 1978) that residents of colonies and other rented areas do not feel the responsibility to show any proprietorial interest in their residential environment, and thus UCD programmes located in such milieux tend to be relatively ineffective. By contrast, slum and spontaneous settlement dwellers, despite the often precarious nature of their land rights, will reveal a much greater potential for taking an interest in local improvements, once stimulated. (Unsurprisingly, for India, one can also find statements to the contrary).

142

3. RESIDENTS' PERCEPTIONS

As previously mentioned, even in western
society the relationship between, and
efficacy of, concepts of 'community' and
territorial affiliation, has at best been seen
as questionable. While such observers as
Everitt (1976) have admitted that possibly no
social context is without some spatial
connotation, many structural aspects of
relationships, attitudes and values are not
necessarily constrained by spatial
considerations. This has been referred to as
the 'less-place' realm, as distinct from the
misconception of 'non-place' aspatial contexts
(section 4.1).

Nevertheless, the local residential area, as
an action space for the poor, unemployed,
retired, young and housewives, is still
considered an important milieu in relatively
mobile western society. Thus conventional
wisdom might suggest that the impoverished
Indian urban resident would value spatial
proximity in his day-to-day life even more :
witness the pavement dweller sleeping close to
his place of work.

But this argument side-steps two
interrelated constraints : the ephemeral
relationship between space and community and
the lack of a 'community' concept in Indian
urban residential development. The high degree
of rural to urban migration in Indian society,
and the relatively strong links maintained
between the milieux is emphasised by urban
slum dwellers' allegiance to kin/village/
regional/linguistic considerations rather than
necessarily to those of residential proximity.
The government chief planner, for example, has
suggested that only with second or even third
generation urban dwellers will urban values
be sufficiently developed to fully take
advantage of UCD programmes (Chandrashekhara,
1978). Indeed, this has been symbolised by the
phenomenon of return migration, emphasising
what would appear to be the rural migrant's lack
of emotional attachment to the city. Evidence
from Bombay has revealed that of in-migrants
over 34 years of age, 60% left again within
four years, while the proportion for those
over 55 years was a remarkably high 76%
(Zachariah, 1966). A number of different
categories of migrants appeared to fall into
this pattern: visitors; transferred government
servants; mill workers and other unskilled
manual groups returning to agricultural
cultivation after ten to fifteen years in the
city; retired workers going 'home'; wives and
children of low income workers returning to
the lower cost more congenial villages; and
those migrants unable to find suitable jobs in
the city. Census data are, however, rather
insufficient in answering a number of
questions in this field (Zachariah, 1966).

It could well be suggested, therefore that
low income groups may be just as physically

mobile as higher income groups, if not more so, but they are highly constrained by traditional socio-cultural structures in terms of social mobility. Turner, (1968) in work on Lima, Peru, suggested that as a migrant's situation as an urban dweller changes, so too do the priorities determining his dwelling environment. Thus a model might suggest a first stage of staying with relatives or street sleeping, reflecting the need for ecomony before the migrant has found employment. Later, with gainful employment and family reunion, he might rent space in a city centre slum to provide shelter for his nuclear family while also maintaining accessibility to his employment. Finally, with increasing income and job security, Turner suggested that the migrant would move with his family to a spontaneous settlement area, his own 'acceptance' within the city being reflected in dwelling 'ownership' and status.

One can see, however, that this model, emphasising low status physical mobility, and reflecting the lack of strong association with residential neighbourhood per se, is just one of a number of alternatives. Benninger (1970) for example, has suggested for the poor urban dweller of South East Asian cities, that in addition to these three 'stages', which he refers to as the 'reception', 'intermediate' and 'consolidated' 'situations', a 'prolonged reception' situation may also persist where a migrant's condition continues to remain the same, reflecting a failure to integrate into the economic and/or social environment, either remaining unemployed or perhaps engaged in casual manual labour or in very marginal retailing. Thus street sleeping, albeit on a more institutionalised basis, may be maintained as the only viable form of accommodation in terms of cost and potential accessibility to jobs and markets.

Benninger further goes on to suggest that, emphasising the wide range of socio-cultural and economic environments impinging upon residential location both within and between Indian cities, a number of models could be suggested for patterns of movement and time scales relating to his four situations. Thus while an 'incremental' pattern from reception through intermediate to the consolidated stage can be referred to as the optimal model, other permutations of these situations can be experienced.

Emphasising, therefore, the rather ephemeral relationship between residential space and emotional attachment, the absence of a notion of 'community' within urban residential development further constrains efforts to establish self-help and mutual aid schemes under banners declaring UCD. Indeed, it was suggested to the writer on more than one occasion that the term 'community development' not only possessed little cultural meaning, but with oblique activities undertaken during the

country's period of emergency rule (June 26th.
1975 to March 21st. 1977), it had accrued a
rather pejorative connotation, such that urban
'renewal' and rural development were being
employed as replacement terms within their
respective milieux.

4. SOCIAL AND ECONOMIC INTERACTION

A tradition amongst geographers has been
the analysis of spatial variables to determine
service areas revealing relative spheres of
influence and hierarchical patterns of a wide
range of functional structures. Spatial
delimitation of urban neighbourhoods for UCD
purposes might be thought of as suggesting a
similar approach. The cultural particularities
of Indian urban life, however, tend to
militate against such apparently easy
demarcation, and further constrain UCD policy.
Unplanned slum and spontaneous settlement
areas rarely reveal morphological
characteristics analogous to formalised
neighbourhoods.
Certainly local residents will be aware of
'cultural divides' within the urban fabric, but
spatial segregation and differentiation per se
may be symbolic and psychological rather than
tangibly morphological. This is particularly
important if bureaucratic decision makers are
intent on rigidly defining boundaries
according to (what might be for them, perhaps
strangers to the area in question) apparently
obvious morphological characteristics (see 1
above). Moreover, social and economic patterns,
however spatially related, are dynamic and may
change rapidly in time, whereas urban
morphology, even in India, is relatively
inflexible in trying to adapt to such changes.
This is further buttressed by the prevalence
of the informal economic sector, within which
probably a large proportion of slum dwellers
will be operating - the proto-proletariat in
McGee's (1976) terminology. Within this sector
activities are not necessarily restricted by
legal constraints. Questions of health and
safety, child labour, sub-contracting, bribery
and protection aid the submergence of the
informal sector into a statistically
inconsistent and spatially ill-defined web of
relationships and bonds transcending any formal
notions of service areas or labour sheds.

5. LOCAL LEADERS

A prerequisite for self-help and mutual aid
approaches is the emergence of indigenous,
locally recognised leaders. Initially in a UCD
programme, surveys may be carried out putting
questions to residents designed to focus upon
the presence of pivotal figures in the
everyday life of urban localities ("who would
you go to locally...." etc.). Once the leader
has been recognised, established, nurtured and
given appropriate responsibility, the

conventional wisdom states that UCD agencies can then quietly withdraw allowing residents, through their leader, to carry on the dynamism of the existing programme, with perhaps simply some financial and infrastructural support continuing from external sources.

A number of potential constraints raise themselves here. Perhaps the most obvious is that which embarrasingly reveals itself when no local leader is forthcoming, as happened in a number of cases in Delhi (Chandrashekhara, 1978) 1978). If the agency has planned or undertaken to withdraw by a certain date, can an artificial, unrepresentative 'leader' be plucked out from the resident body? Similarly, of only a weak or inarticulate leader is forthcoming, can the withdrawing agency place its reliance in him and act in the best interests of the local community? Conversely, a strong leader may emerge who, with the status of representing the local population, strongly opposes either in outline or detail, the approach taken by the withdrawing agency in its overall programme, perhaps reflecting conflicting perceptions of the nature and purpose of UCD.

Finally, a common problematical constraint is the emergence of two or more local leaders with conflicting perceptions of local needs with perhaps bases of support in different parts of the same area. Such a situation can reflect 'inappropriate' bounding of an area in relation to its socio-cultural characteristics, and a potential solution may therefore be a sub-division of the area or a boundary revision. On the other hand, if the spatially based support for two or more mutually exclusive leaders is not clear cut, then major constraining problems present themselves.

But again, dynamic social processes will not allow any given situation to remain constant. Any of the above examples can arise and just as quickly disappear again as the spatial expression of socio-political relationships undergoes modification.

6. PRE-EXISTING VOLUNTARY ASSOCIATIONS

As noted in chapter 6, divergent approaches have been taken by UCD agencies in respect of the presence or otherwise of pre-existing voluntary organisations. The Indo-Dutch Project in Hyderabad (section 6.2.3) concentrates upon areas devoid of such mechanisms, whereas the Municipal Corporation of Hyderabad (6.2.1/2) tends to work in just those areas containing such bodies, arguing that they reflect evidence of local interest and a dynamism of aims which can be built upon and consolidated. The Indo-Dutch argument, by contrast, emphasises that those impoverished areas without such pre-existing mechanisms are likely, not least because of such an absence, to be those in most need.

Certainly this dichotomy reflects in some
measure the problem of the so-called 'inverse
care law' (Duncan, 1974; Brooks, 1975; also
section 4.4 above) whereby bureaucratically
controlled resources may be channelled into
those areas and problems which are easiest to
redeem and can show relatively rapid results,
rather than going to help those with the most
pressing and intransigent problems.

A major constraint imposed by the pre-
existence of voluntary organisations within an
area formally designated for UCD, is the spatial
correspondence between such organisations and
the specific area in question. If multiple
organisations, pursuing similar functions
exist, potential conflicts of aim may arise
between them, and indeed, between them and the
UCD agency. The organisations may be competing
for limited resources in the same area, or one
may overlap adjacent areas whose resource needs,
it might be argued, are equally pressing,
thereby stimulating a demand for inclusion and
boundary revision of the UCD area.

7. SUITABLE PREMISES

The lack of availability of a meeting place,
community hall or central focal point is an
obvious physical constraint. In many projects,
such as in Delhi and Hyderabad, high priority
has been given to the establishment of such
institutional features. Within inner city
slums, such as Shahjahanabad in Delhi or
Patthargatti in Hyderabad (Fig 6.1) the
constraints on available space or the ability
to convert existing premises to such use are
paramount.

The potential conflict of aims between levels
of administration and short term changes in
policy can impinge upon the effectiveness and
relevance of institutional buildings for UCD
purposes. Thus Delhi Municipal Corporation
originally established community centres for
its slum dwellers for such socio-economic
pursuits as sewing classes and basket making.
Because of physical constraints on land and the
often complex interdigitation of different
status groups within the Indian urban fabric,
such community centres were often located
adjacent to relatively high status areas. Under
the Indian government's state of emergency
(1975-7) it was Delhi Development Authority's
policy to evict squatters and relocate them in
resettlement colonies on the urban fringes,
particularly in the Trans-Jamuna area to the
east of the city (Fig. 2.4). In this way, many
UCD community centres were deprived of their
original clientele, for whom they were
designed, a situation soon rectified by local,
higher status groups moving into the
organisation of the centres and orientating
them to their own less basic needs :
hairdressing, flower arranging and the like. On
the other hand, initially at least, the new

homes for the relocated slum dwellers, the
resettlement colonies, were devoid of such
centres (Singh, 1978c).

B. 'TRANSCENDANT' CONSTRAINTS

8. ESTABLISHED LOCAL POLITICIANS' ATTITUDES

In a wide range of instances, one constraint
which particularly makes itself felt is the
attitude towards UCD activities held by the
established politicians representing the areas
experiencing UCD programmes. While some measure
of cooperation is usually forthcoming, it is
not difficult to appreciate that some pre-
existing councillors might feel threatened in
their role as local representative by external
agencies entering their 'patch' and perhaps
providing opportunities, incentives and benefits
which the politician may have promised but never
fulfilled. Further, the positive encouragement
of UCD programmes to develop indigenous
leadership from within the area would present
a particularly difficult role conflict to the
politician. Should he aid this process and by
doing so probably reduce his own political
power base, or should he oppose the process
altogether as being anti-democratic and contrary
to established procedures for representative
democracy?

On the other hand, the local leaders encouraged
by UCD programmes, can, and have, often gone on
to establish themselves as political
representatives in higher governmental arenas.
In 1978, for example, the deputy mayor of Delhi
was a former slum dweller who was encouraged by
UCD activities and developed his political
skills out of acting as an indigenous leader
for his local area. In the Naiknagar scheme of
Habitat Hyderabad (section 6.2.2 above), the
resident scheduled tribe of the area revealed
great pride to the present writer over the fact
that one of their sons had gone on to become a
political representative at state government
level. Such examples will have been repeated
throughout the various nation wide UCD
programmes. Do they symbolise a real change in
the power structure, or can one conclude that
such self-help and participation schemes, while
appearing to shift the power balance, are simply
only slightly extending membership of the elite
group power holders?

9. UCD AGENTS

While a large measure of the success or
failure of UCD policy ultimately depends upon
residents' response to the programmes, the
nature and function of UCD agents, working as
catalysts within a spatially defined framework,
would appear crucial, linking external
influences and internal reactions. In their
earlier appraisal of seven Indian UCD projects,
however, Chandra and Punalekar (1975) pointed
to the fact that although each project within

the national programme was authorised for a staff of eight community organisers (four male, four female) and one project officer, none of the projects under study had achieved a full complement of such staff.

As can be seen from Table 7.1, once financial support and impetus from the Ford Foundation had been phased out Delhi's UCD effort actually saw a 50% reduction in its community organisers within three years, with a complete absence of voluntary worker help. By contrast, Hyderabad during this earlier phase, while not included in the very first round of UCD projects, subsequently increased its paid staff to near full capacity, while also pursuing a widespread employment of voluntary workers.

In addition to overall numbers, the standard and quality of staff and sources of recruitment **have** varied quite substantially from one project to another. Generally recognised low pay scales, even by Indian standards, do not take account of housing and inner urban living costs. Consequently, most UCD projects have experienced a relatively high rate of staff turnover, which inevitably reduces the quality of the level of services provided. In addition to poor financial return, UCD staff often experience poor facilities, lack of job security and heavy workloads due to staff shortage, adding to the already strenuous nature of the work.

Supplementation by voluntary workers has rarely been fully realised, yet from experience in Hyderabad, and to a lesser extent Kanpur, it was found that :

"These voluntary workers, wherever recruited and trained, demonstrated remarkable potentials of working as action and change agents in the neighbourhood and provided a functional linkage between the project and the neighbourhood" (Chandra and Punalekar, 1975, 21).

C. 'EXTERNAL' CONSTRAINTS

10. MULTI-LEVEL ADMINISTRATIVE CONTROL

The national UCD programme saw the municipality or corporation directly controlling policy, while in Delhi and Hyderabad for example, the state government exerted influence through its local self government department. Municipal departments were such, however, that on occasion sufficient appreciation and understanding of project needs and problems was not forthcoming, while bureaucratic red tape resulted in unnecessary delays. According to Chandra and Punalekar (1975) some project workers complained about a large part of their time being taken up in municipal duties not forming part of their legitimate role. It was suggested, for example, that officials at the state level did not make sufficient efforts

Table 7.1 Early staff development for selected UCD projects

Year	Aurangabad			Delhi			Hyderabad			Kanpur			Surat		
	PO	CO	VW	PO	CO	VW	PO	CO	VW	PO	CO	VW	PO	CO	VW
1. 1966-7	1	4	9	1	6	–	–	–	–	1	5	–	1	7	–
2. 1967-8	1	4	7	1	5	–	1	4	18	1	4	5	1	6	–
3. 1968-9	1	4	8	1	5	–	1	4	28	1	4	10	1	8	4
4. 1969-70	1	2	7	1	3	–	1	4	41	1	4	14	1	7	8
5. 1970-71	1	1	7	1	3	–	1	4	40	1	4	15	1	6	8
6. 1971-2	1	4	6	1	3	–	1	7	40	1	6	15	1	6	8

PO – Project Officer   CO – Community Organisers   VW – Voluntary Workers

Source : Chandra and Punalekar (1975), 76.

to orientate municipal staff towards the real needs and significance of UCD.

None of the projects studied possessed a director at state level, except in Gujarat, where the position of deputy director was created. But in this particular case the responsible official performed other functions as well as overseeing UCD. Thus, while project staff constantly felt the need for help and guidance from central and state governemnt levels, they seldom received it :

"....heads of municipal and government departments did not have much idea about the urban community development programme and approach and hence could not appreciate and understand the needs and the problems of the projects " (Chandra and Punalkar, 1975, 23).

One major reason for the appointment of a senior directing officer in each state was initially stipulated to be for fostering better understanding and pointing to the functional relationship between various administrative departments and levels. Without a separate UCD director this was rarely achieved. As a consequence, a lack of coordination between administrative staff and field staff has often been pointed to (eg. Kennedy, 1966) with in one case at least the head of a municipal department being shown to have taken more interest in protecting her position than in supporting the UCD programme.

Although most of the country's municipal corporation have appointed UCD officers, the government's chief planner (Chandrashekhara, 1978) agreed that in terms of an overall programme there was not much enthusiasm at municipal and state level. It was suggested that projects has been confused and mixed up with social and welfare programmes such that priorities were never quite established, further reflecting inadequate leadership.

11. EXTERNAL FUNDING

External funding, for example from the Ford Foundation, was instrumental in launching Indian UCD on a reasonable footing, although differing interpretations held between the American and Indian counterparts over what such a programme should entail, slowed down the inaugural process. The constraint it imposed, however, was generally one of relative apathy and undue reliance on the part of the Indian cooperating body. Thus in Delhi when Ford Foundation support was phased out, financial and moral support from the Delhi authorities could not compensate, and the programme lapsed into relative decline. Such a client relationship, while arguably beneficial in the long term, brought about a number of short term constraints. The Indo-Dutch approach by comparison, emphasised that it was not a

charity and that residents taking part would be
required to contribute - in money, goods or
effort. This would seem a sensible approach,
requiring contributory participation from those
who wanted to benefit.

7.3. GEOGRAPHICAL IMPLICATIONS FOR PUBLIC
   POLICY

"Space clearly plays an important role in
social processes.....(but)... too much recent
human geography has erred in neglecting the
social, economic, and political aspects of its
object of study..." (Hamnett, 1979, 245).

".....what is necessary rather, is to show how
space and other material elements of social
organization are articulated within a coherent
theoretical or conceptual whole" (Castells,
1976, 30).

Such a framework has been attempted in this
chapter, focussing upon the constraints likely
to modify UCD policies as they affect specific
areas. But such a spatial approach, especially
in its relatively localised form, does avoid a
number of questions which are not easy to
accommodate in any purely geographical
framework.
Rarely has the analysis questioned the
underlying motives, assumptions and fundamental
principles of UCD policy itself. One particular
ideological approach would argue that such a
policy is bound to fail because it is largely
working within the status quo and is not
significantly transforming the social structure
and the root causes of many (localised) problems
inherent in such a structure. Thus for example,
while the ethos of self-help and cooperation
might demand the coming together of different
caste and sub-caste groups for their mutual
benefit, in practice UCD policy is not likely
to have the slightest effect on India's caste
system overall. At the local level, by virtue
of the fact that UCD programme areas need some
degree of social homogeneity to be successful
(as spelt out in a number of policy guidelines)
boundaries are most likely to be drawn between
caste and sub-caste groups- rather than bringing
them together. But even where such areas do
include different groups, and even if they do
successfully undertake mutual cooperation to the
extent of reducing caste friction, the impact of
such individual, localised patterns on a system
based on an all-embracing national tradition is
still likely to be minimal.
At the personal level, while caste is less
important in urban areas for friendhsip ties, it
still performs a paramount role in marriages.
Again, while in many urban jobs, particularly in
the tertiary sector, there are few caste
equivalents (the caste system having developed
from rural pursuits), there still exists an
implicit caste-linked hierarchy in the non -

manual sector. This may be explicitly
manifested in terms of literacy, education and
language. In urban political associations caste
still plays an important role also (Khatu,
1978c), and UCD workers themselves are just as
likely to hold their own caste or religious
biases.

While the persistence of the notion of
ritual pollution is reduced by the high
densities, close proximity, heterogeneity and
the communal nature of urban slum living,
because many policies affect the relatively
large Harijan ('untouchable') group, positive
discriminatory policies might be thought of by
other caste groups as simply setting the
Harijans further apart. Certainly in the rural
sector, anti-Harijan riots have been a familiar
feature, particularly in the north of the
country, in the wake of governmental attempts
to provide this deprived group with some
agricultrual land of their own.

A further ideological stance which could be
taken is that which states that by specifically
designating localised areas for UCD programmes,
an internally imperialistic 'divide and rule'
mentality is being enacted. That by spatially
and functionally closing off one social sub-
system from another, the great Indian (urban)
masses are being denied an overall voice, a
voice and a strength which could challenge and
supplant the existing socio-political system.
By demarcating specific areas and localising
policies one is simply denying wider
aspirations and indeed increasing
differentiation between demarcated and non-
demarcated areas. (As revealed in Hyderabad
(section 6.2.2), rather than feeling stigmatised
by having their residential area referred to as
a slum, residents were usually eager to be
included in such a demarcated area in order to
benefit from the resource inputs accruing to
improve such slums).

As previously noted, Hyderabad might well be
pointed to as one of the more enlightened
authorities, in that, realising the
impossibility of attempting to encapsulate a
'concentration' of social problems within any
given city area, it is now attempting to pursue
a far more 'less spatial' approach, being
willing (with , it must be admitted, UNICEF
help) to assess and operate policies within any
part of its authorised area.

Thus Hyderabad has broken away from the
relative regidity which appeared to constrain
a number of the earlier projects within the
national programme. Such a rigidity is perhaps
inherent within the Indian bureaucratic system
(whereby clerical jobs may involve no more than
shuffling back into order piles of papers blown
into disarray by the ever whirring ceiling fan).
The demise of projects in Goa, Rajasthan, Uttar
Pradesh and West Bengal early in the programme's
development (Table 5.4) reflected bureaucratic
inertia especially at the state level. But also

affecting these projects was, and still is, the
overall constraint of the availability of
finance:

".....in many cases action in approving the
start of a project was delayed and some of the
States even abandoned the idea of sponsoring
any project because of the difficulties in
getting clearance of their respective Finance
Departments due to constraint of resources"
(Chandra and Punalekar, 1975, 7.)

Such macro-level constraints, without a close
examination of national and state allocation
policies, cannot be adequately accommodated
within a purely spatial frame. They derive
from national, or indeed international
contexts. the complexity of which is outside
the scope of this monograph.

In breaking away from the early rigidity,
Hyderabad was perhaps inspired by developments
at Baroda. The effects of such cross-
fertilisation are, of course, difficult to
measure and assess. While Baroda, especially
from 1969 onwards, demonstrated the possibility
of an alternative UCD administrative structure
(section 6.3) its unique origins have rendered
any specific replication difficult. The Indo-
Dutch Project again reflects a further stance,
developing on a modest scale from an initial
rural programme (section 6.2.3), and being
self-supporting to the extent of 60% costs,
with the remainder shared equally between
Hyderabad Municipal Corporation, the state
health department, local institutions and the
community itself (Butt, 1978).

Under the circumstances of such
administrative diversity, is it appropriate to
refer to an Indian UCD policy? Rather, there
appear to be a number of policies, or at least
agencies, which, while pursuing largely similar
long term objectives, have approached these
objectives through differing methods, as
exemplified in chapter 6. The size and
diversity of India would suggest that this is
only realistic.

A final point to make about the spatial
significance of UCD policy concerns the time
dimension. As has been repeated previously,
with the dynamic nature of social processes,
spatially expressed patterns of Indian urban
life will inevitably change not only in relation
to a whole range of variables, but also
to their different time scales - daily/ weekly
modifications (eg. social networks), longer
term change (employment patterns, redevelopment
and land use change), continuous processes
(accretion/contraction of spontaneous
settlements, mobility of pavement dwellers),
patterns of seasonal climatic influence
(floods, drought, frosts) and even isolated
tectonic effects (eathquakes). The question
therefore needs to be asked as to the efficacy
of any static area delimitation in the face of

such dynamic urban processes. It can be argued (section 4.1 above) that if a contiguous area is designated for a specific purpose, then this may help to localise certain functions and stimulate the growth of a community attitude (Poplin, 1972). But not all dynamic processes are likely to be modified by such an imposition, even when it is a relatively comprehensive UCD policy.

7.4 CONCLUSIONS

Looking to the future one can forsee increasing international interest in Third World UCD. Building on work stimulated by the Ford Foundation (the Mukherjee-Davies Plan), Calcutta, perhaps unfairly neglected in this monograph, has seen a channelling of overseas aid into its Bustee Development Organisation. Formed by an amalgamation of voluntary groups in 1974, this body began to receive aid from the newly established Europe-Calcutta Consortium. Involving such groups as Christian Aid, the Consortium helped sponsor a four year programme of bustee improvement in 1975 (Sivaramkrishnan, 1977a). European church agencies have also been supporting city slum improvement through a forum of twenty-five voluntary organisations - the Calcutta Urban Service Consortium. The World Bank (1979) also lays claim to altruism in relation to Third World slum areas, having 'invested' $1,100 million in 42 urban development projects affecting six million people since 1972. But how far is Wiebe correct when he states :

"emphases in dealing with the more disadvantaged are usually placed on attempts to alleviate the problem such people pose for the better off" (Wiebe, 1977, 213).

The flurry of idealism which saw Indian UCD projects take off in the 1960s, however, has inevitably, and realistically, dissipated itself. Notwithstanding enlightened self-build home programmes (eg. Habitat Hyderabad), demolition programmes and the depredations of the national emergency, there has grown an (often reluctant) acceptance that slums and spontaneous settlements are a permanent and growing aspect of the urban environment. However comprehensive the earlier UCD programmes were intended to be, financial constraints and a strengthening pragmatism have evolved relatively low key approaches relying heavily upon self-help and minimum inputs.

One point has become clear. The importance of economic programmes within UCD schemes cannot be overestimated. Skill enhancement, job referral schemes, female based cottage industries and even the production of protein packets for a small profit (section 6.2.3)

must be seen as vital in raising the pitifull
income levels of slum dwellers, and by so doing
raising their levels of expectation, modifying
their social and cultural attitudes (eg.
towards family planning) and helping to
gradually remove the 'slum mentality'. Any
Indian slum UCD project without an economic
enhancement component is not worth commencing.

Complementing economic enhancement, however,
is the need to make residents aware of their
contribution to society through refusing to
give them charity status. The Indo-Dutch
Project in Hyderabad demanded participation in
terms of money goods or labour. This both
reduces any possible stigma, brings a degree
of reciprocity to the development process and
helps to stimulate self-esteem.

With increasing financial pressure, the role
of voluntary workers, and self-help is even
more important. As was shown in relation to the
original formal UCD projects (eg. Table 7.1)
the take up of voluntary help to supplement full
time community workers was generally
insufficient. Future trends will dictate a much
fuller use of such a resource.

Conclusions can now be summarised with
questions posed for further debate.

    1. UCD programmes are not intended to
fundamentally transform the structure of Indian
society. Can the problems which such policies
are attempting to tackle ever begin to be
eradicated without basic structural change?

    2. It can be argued that rather than aiding
urban localities, by demarcating specific areas
of operation for UCD and pursuing a policy of
positive discrimination, a 'divide and rule'
ethos may be seen to have been imposed upon the
Indian urban population to weld it firmly to the
status quo. Is this a healthy trend to pursue?
Will it survive intact as such?

    3. Nationally and internationally derived
financial constraints override most localised
factors exemplified in chapter 6 and section
7.2. What priorities, therefore, should be
given for adequately financing UCD projects?
Will their perceived worth decline even further
than it has already?

    4. Mindful of these pre-conditions, a wide
range of social, economic, political and
physical constraints exert themselves at the
local level to modify the actual application of
any stated UCD policy. It is at this level that
spatial analysis appears to be most apposite.
Yet as many of these constraints are culture
specific, indigenous to Indian social life,
applications of 'western' based analytical
models are only partially meaningful. For
example, in relation to the employment of
factorial ecology in Indian urban analysis

"....the approach has come under attack for
conceptual, methodological and other
shortcomings, (but) it continues to have its
utility as a part of certain theoretical
orientations" (Weinstein and Pillai, 1979,205).

The employment of a constraint model,
therefore, allowed a flexibility in conceptual
approach to accommodate empirical indigenous
factors amenable to spatial analysis.

As stated in the introduction (section 1.2)
the major immediate conclusion arising out of
this monograph points to the fact that because
of India's spatially expressed diversity at
national, regional, urban and neighbourhood levels,
no one policy so rooted in cultural values as
UCD can hope to be applied with anything
resembling uniformity over the country's
myriad and heterogeneous urban areas. But even
more pertinently, is it an appropriate approach
within which to bring improvements to that
diversity?

In their earlier evaluation of a number of
the national programmes projects, Chandra and
Punalekar (1975) enumerated those areas in
which they saw future evaluation being most
appropriate :

"(a) identification of community
characteristics and local factors that help or
hinder community participation;

(b) varying factors arising out of
sponsorship and agency organisation for the
development of the programme;

(c) administrative problems and procedures
and the manner of coordination at different
levels; and

(d) impact of different kinds of programmes
and community reactions under varying socio-
economic conditions" (Chandra and Punalekar,
1975, 106).

While this short monograph has not been able
to explore these avenues with much more than a
cursory glance, it has been able to point to a
society whose spatially expressed social
and morphologiacl structure contains
fundamental differences from those of western
experience. But the differentiation and
inequalities which appear so entrenched in
Indian society suggest that any social policy
short of fundamental structural change may
bring little long term benefit. Certainly UCD
programmes have their place. At the present
time they represent a small number of people
attempting a mammoth task producing modest
success in the face of profound endemic
constraints. In isolation such attempts appear
as palliatives, piecemeal and vainglorious,
however well intentioned. In tandem with major
structural changes, however, an altogether
different picture might emerge.

In the face of so much urban and rural deprivation, both relative and absolute, it is worth finally reflecting on the fact that India is extremely rich in resources – minerals, energy, water and cultivable land, with a lower overall population density than the United Kingdon. Indeed,

"India is actually capable of economic self-sufficiency" (Selbourne, 1977, 2; Government of India, 1975, 11).

Appendix-Glossary of Indian Terms

BALWADI : nursery

CHAUK/CHOWK : main bazaar

'ECONOMICALLY WEAKER' : usually applied to unemployed members of Indian society and who thus are faced with major problems in obtaining accommodation

GRAM SEVAK : village level (community development) worker

GURUDWARA : Sikh temple

KAKAIYA : sun dried bricks

KATCHA : temporary and flimsy (building materials)

'LOWER INCOME GROUPS' : usually referring to employed persons with low incomes, who, for accommodation purposes, may need to ascertain certification from their employer to confirm a regular income

MAHILA (MOHILA) SAMITI : women's organisation/club

MOHALLA : neighbourhood/ward

PANCHAYAT : literally a council of five; the basic participatory unit of village government

PANCHAYATI RAJ : the system of rural local government

PANCHAYAT SAMITI : body comprising the chairmen of village panchayats and acting as the principle unit of rural local government

PATTAS : land rights

PUCCA : permanent and strong (building materials)

VIKAS MANDAL : urban citizens' (community) development council

VIKAS PARISHAD : urban neighbourhood council

VIKAS SABHA : urban 'zone' councils

ZILA PARISHAD : body comprising panchayat
samiti chairmen.

Bibliography

AGARWALA, S.N. (1958) A method for estimating decade internal migration in cities from Indian data Indian Econ. Rev., 4, 59-76.

AHMAD, Q. (1965) Indian cities : characteristics and correlates Univ. Chicago, Dept. Geog., Res. Pap. 102.

ALAM, S.M. (1963) Commercial structure of the cities of Hyderabad-Secunderabad Journ. Osmania Univ., 1.
        (1965) Hyderabad-Secunderabad (twin cities): a study in urban geography Allied Publishers.
        (1969) Metropolitan Hyderabad and its region. Rep. of the Hyderabad Res. Proj., Osmania Univ.
        (1971) Two cultures urite in Hyderabad Geog. Mag., 43(6), 409-416.
        & W.KHAN (1972) Metropolitan Hyderabad and its region Asia Publishing house.

AMES, M.M. (1968) Modernization and social structure in Jamshedpur Development Digest, 6, 55-61.

ARANGANNAL, R. (1975) Socio-economic survey of Madras slums Tamil Nadu Slum Clearance Board.

ARGAL, R. (1955) Municipal government in India Agarwal Press.

ASHRAF, A. (1967) The city government of Calcutta : a study cf inertia Asia Publishing House.
        & L. GREEN (1972) Calcutta. In ROBSON, W.A. & D.E. REGAN (EDS) Great cities of the world : their government, politics and planning Allen & Unwin, 297-330.

BARODA CITIZENS COUNCIL (1974) Memorandum and articles of association.

BAXTER, R. (1974) New Bombay - the twin city Geogr., 59, 51-54.

BELLWINKEL, M. (1973) Rajasthani contract labour in Delhi Sociol. Bull., 22(1).

BENNINGER, C. (1970) Models of Habitat mobility in transitional economies Ekistics, 29(171), 124-127.
        (1972) Design criteria for developing contexts : housing for Baroda Ekistics, 33, 162-165.

162

BERREMAN, G.D. (1963) Caste and community development Human Organization, 22, 90-94.

BERRY, B.J.L. & P.H. REES (1969) The factorial ecology of Calcutta Amer. Journ. Sociol., 74, 445-491.

BERRY, B.J.L. & H. SPODECK (1971) Comparative ecologies of large Indian cities Econ. Geogr., 47(2) (Supp.), 266-285. Reprinted in SCHWIRIAN, K.P. (ED) (1974) Comparative urban structure D.C. Heath, 349-370.

BHARAT SEVAK SAMAJ, DELHI PRADESH (1958) Slums of Old Delhi Atma Ram & Sons.

BHAT, L.S. (1972) Regional planning in India Statistical Publishing Society, Calcutta.

BHATIA, S.S. (1956) Historical geography of Delhi Indian Geographer, 1, 17-43.

BHATT, M. & V.K. CHAWDA (1972) The anatomy of urban poverty Gujarat University.

BHATTACHARYA, M. (1971) Urban local government Perspectives, supp. to Indian Journ. Public Admin. , 17(4).
        (1972) Inter-governmental relations in municipal welfare services Nagarlok, 4(4), 31-35.

BLAIR, D.J. & T.H. BISS (1967) The measurement of shape in geography Univ.Nottingham, Dept. Geog.

BODAS, V.V. ET AL (1969) Housing problems in Delhi Journ. Inst. Town Plann. (India), 58, 46-55.

BOGAERT, M. Van Den (1977) Entrepreneurial patterns in the urban informal sector : the case of tribal entrepreneurs in Ranchi Social Action, 27(3), 306-323.

BOGUE, D.J. & K.C. ZACHARIAH (1962) Urbanization and migration in India. In TURNER, R. (ED) India's urban future Univ. California Press, 27-54.

BOPEGAMAGE, A. (1957) Delhi : a study in urban sociology Univ. Bombay.

BOSE, A. (1966) Studies in India's urbanization Institute of Economic Growth, New Delhi.
    (1970) Urbanization in India : an inventory of source materials Academic Books, Bombay.
    (1976) Bibliography on urbanization in India 1947-1976 Tata McGraw-Hill.
    (1978) India's urbanization 1901-2001 Tata McGraw-Hill, 2nd. ed.
    (ED)(1974) Population in India's development Vikas.
        (1977) Population statistics in India Vikas.

BOSE, N.K. (1965) Calcutta : a pre-mature
    metropolis Scientific Amer. 213(3), 90-
    102.

BREESE, G. (1963) Urban development problems in
    India Annals Assoc. Amer. Geogrs., 53,
    253-265.

BREESE, G. (1974) Urban and regional planning
    for Delhi-New Delhi Princeton Univ.
    Press.

BRUSH, J.E. (1962) The morphology of Indian
    cities. In, TURNER, R. (ED) India's
    urban future Univ. California Press, 57-
    70.
        (1968) Spatial patterns of
    population in Indian cities Geogr. Rev.,
    58, 362-391. Reprinted in DWYER, D.J.
    (ED) (1974) The city in the third world
    Macmillan, 105-132.
        (1975) Elite residential colonies
    Dept. Geog., Rutgers Univ., New Jersey.
    Mimeo.

BULSARA, J.F. (1964) Problems of rapid
    urbanisation in India Popular Prakashan.

BUTT, H. (1978) Personal interviews Chairman,
    Indo-Dutch Project for Child Welfare and
    Nutrition, Hyderabad.

CAPLAN, A.P. (1977) A study of selected
    women's organisations in Madras City.
    SSRC Rep. HR2908.

CAPLAN, L. (1978) An anthropological study of
    Christian elites in urban south India
    SSRC Rep. HR3171.

CASTELLS, M. (1976) Theoretical propositions
    for an experimental study of urban social
    movements. In PICKVANCE, C.G. (ED) Urban
    sociology : critical essays Tavistock,
    147-173.

CENSUS OF INDIA 1971

CHAKRAVORTY, S. (1975) Farm women labour :
    waste and exploitation Social change ,
    5(1-2).

CHANDER, J.P. (1969) Delhi : a political study
    Metropolitan, Delhi.

CHANDRA, S. & S.P. PUNALEKAR (1975) Urban
    community development programme in India
    National Institute of Public Cooperation
    & Child Development.

CHANDRASHEKHARA, C.S. (1978) Personal interviews
    Chief Planner, Town & Country Planning
    Organisation, Government of India.

CHATTERJEE, B. (1961) India applies rural
    techniques of self help to rapidly
    growing city neighbourhoods Journ. of
    Housing, 18, 193-197.
        (1962a) The Delhi urban
    community development project Ford
    Foundation Program Letter, 130.

164

(1962b) Urban community development : Delhi Project : a review *Indian Journ. of Social Work*, Oct.

(1975) Foreward. In CHANDRA, S. & S.P. PUNALEKAR *Urban community development programme in India* National Institute of Public Cooperation & Child Development.

(1978) *Personal interview* Director, National Institute of Public Cooperation & Child Development.

& M.B. CLINARD (1961) *Organizing citizens' development councils (Vikas mandals)* Dept. of Urban Community Development, Municipal Corporation of Delhi.

CHOPRA, P. (1970) *Delhi : history and places of interest* Delhi Administration.

CHOWDHRY, D.P. (1971) *Voluntary social welfare in India* Sterling Press.

CLINARD, M.B. (1961) The Delhi Pilot Project in urban community development *Internat. Rev. of Community Dev.*, 7, 161-171.

(1966) *Slums and community development* Free Press.

& B. CHATTERJEE (1962) urban community development in India : the Delhi Pilot Project. In TURNER, R. (ED) *India's urban future* Univ.California Press, 71-93.

COUSINS, W.J. (1978a) *People's participation in the development of small and medium sized towns* Pap. given at Quaker Seminar, 'Small and medium sized towns in regional development', Kathmandhu.

(1978b) *Personal interview* UNICEF Urban Affairs Officer for India.

CRANE, R. (1954) Urbanism in India *Amer. Journ. Sociol.*, 60, 463-470.

DALAL, N. (1973) Cities and towns of India, 5: Hyderabad : where cultures meet *Times Weekly* (India), April 29th.

DASGUPTA, B. (1971) Socio-economic classification of districts : a statistical approach *Economic & Political Weekly* (India), 6 (33).

& R. LAISLEY (1975) Migration from villages *Econ. & Polit. Weekly* , 10 (42).

DATTA, A. (1978a) *Personel interview* Professor of Urban Administration & Development Municipal Finance, Indian Institute of Public Administration.

(1978b) *Training for slum improvement and squatter settlements : an Indian viewpoint* Pap. presented at U.N. Expert Group Meeting on Training Programme on the Improvement of Slums and Squatter Areas in Rural and Urban Communities, Enschede.

& J.N. KHOSLA (1972) Delhi. In
ROBSON, W.A. & D.E. REGAN (EDS) Great
cities of the world : their government,
politics and planning Allen & Unwin, 2
vols., 3rd. ed.

DELHI ADMINISTRATION, BUREAU OF ECONOMICS &
STATISTICS (1970) Delhi statistical handbook
1970 Delhi Administration

DELHI ADMINISTRATION, PLANNING DEPARTMENT
(1968) Draft fourth five-year plan (1969-
70 to 1973-74) Delhi Administration.

DELHI DEVELOPMENT AUTHORITY (1961) Master plan
and work studies for Delhi D.D.A., 2 vols.

DELHI IMPROVEMENT TRUST ENQUIRY COMMITTEE (1951)
Report Govt. of India Press.

DELHI SCHOOL OF SOCIAL WORK (1959) The beggar
problem in metropolitan Delhi D.S.S.W.

DEPARTMENT OF THE ENVIRONMENT (1974)
Neighbourhood councils in England
Consultation Pap.

DEPARTMENT OF URBAN COMMUNITY DEVELOPMENT,
DELHI MUNICIPAL CORPORATION (1959)
Manual for urban community organizers
D.M.C.
                        (1961a)
Organizing citizens' development councils
D.M.C.
                        (1961b)
Urban community development in Delhi :
pilot project 1958-60 D.M.C.
                        (1962)
Evaluation study of the vikas mandals
(citizens' development councils) D.M.C.

DESAI, A.R. (1969) Rural sociology in India
Indian Society of Agricultural Economics.
            & S.D. PILLAI (1972) A profile of
an Indian slum Univ. of Bombay.

DESHMUKH, M.B. (1956) Delhi : a study of
floating migration. In TEXTOR, R.B. ET AL
The social implications of
industrialization and urbanization UNESCO,
143-225.

DESHPANDE, C.D. & L.S. BHAT (1975) India. In
JONES, R. (ED) Essays on world population
Philip, 358-376.

DE SOUZA , A. (1978) Personal interview Director
of Research, Indian Social Institute.

DHEKNEY, B.R. (1959) Hubli city : a study in
urban economic life Dharwar.

D'SOUZA, V.S. (1975) Scheduled castes and
urbanisation in Punjab : an explanation
Sociol. Bull., 24(1).
            (1968) Social structure of a
planned city - Chandigarh Orient-Longman.

DUBE, S.C. (1955) Indian village Routledge &
Kegan Paul.

DWYER, D.J. (1975) People and housing in third world cities Longman.
    (1978) The third world city Geogr. Mag., 50(8), 519-522.
    (ED).(1972) The city as a centre of change in Asia Hong Kong Univ. Press.
    (1974) The city in the third world Macmillan.

EAMES, E. (1967) Urban migration and the joint family in a North Indian village Journ. Developing Areas, 1, 163-177.
    (1970) Corporate groups and Indian urbanization Anthropological Quart., 43, 165-186.

ELDERSVELD, S.J. ET AL (1968) The citizen and the administrator in a developing democracy : an empirical study in Delhi state Indian Institute of Public Administration.

EVERITT, J.C. (1976) Community and propinquity in a city Annals Assoc. Amer. Geogrs. , 66, 104-116.

EWING, J.R. (1969) Town planning in Delhi : a critique Econ. & Polit. Weekly, 4(40), 1591-1600.

FIREY, W. (1947) Land use in central Boston Harvard Univ. Press.

FONSECA, R. (1969) The walled city of Old Delhi. In OLIVER, P. (ED) Shelter and society Cresset Press.
    (1970) The walled city of Old Delhi: urban renewal and an indigenous community Landscape, 8(8), 15-35.
    (1971) The walled city of Delhi Ekistics, 31(182), 72-80.

FRANK, A.G. (1969) Latin America : underdevelopment or revolution New York .

FRIEDMANN, J. & R. WULFF (1976) The urban transition : comparative studies of newly industrializing societies Arnold.

GADGIL, D.R. (1945) Poona : a socio-economic survey Part 1 Gokhale Institute of Politics & Economics, Pune, Pub. No. 12.
    (1952) Poona : a socio-economic survey. Part II Gokhale Institute of Politics & Economics, Pune, Pub. No. 25.
    (1965) Sholapur city : socio - economic studies Gokhale Institute of Politics & Economics, Pune.

GANGULI, B.N. (1973) Gandhi's social philosophy Vikas.

GERMANI, G. (1967) The concept of social integration. In BEYER,G. (ED), The urban explosion in Latin America Cornell Univ. Press, 175-188.

GHURYE, G.S. (1963) Anatomy of a rururban community Popular Prakashan.

GILLION, K. (1968) Ahmedabad : a study in Indian urban history Univ. California Press.

GINSBURG, N.S. (1965) Urban geography and 'non-western' areas. In HAUSER, P. & L.F. SCHNORE (EDS) The study of urbanization Wiley, 311-346. Reprinted in BREESE, G. (ED) (1969) The city in newly developing countries Prentice Hall, 409-435.

GIST, N.P. (1957) The ecology of Bangalore, India : an east-west comparison Social Forces, 35, 356-365.
        (1958) The ecological structure of an Asian city (Bangalore) : an east-west comparison Population Rev., 2, 17-25.

GOSAL, G.S. (1962) Regional aspects of population growth in India, 1951-61 Pacific Viewpoint, 3, 87-99.
        (1974) Population growth in India, 1961-1971 : a spatial perspective Asian Profile, 2, 193-212.

GOULD, H.A. (1965) Lucknow rickshawallas : the social organization of an occupational category Internatl. Journ. Comparative Sociol., 6, 24-47.

GOVERNMENT OF INDIA (1975) A hundred new gains Ministry of Information & Broadcasting.

GUPTA, J.D. & B.G. HUTCHINSON (1979) Regional-development optimization for the Delhi region of India Environment & Plann. , A, 11, 435-446.

HALL, D.R. (1978) A geographical study of social divisions in Portsmouth Univ. London, unpub. Ph.D.
        (1979) Community and behaviour in urban environments. In GURKAYNAK, M. & A. LECOMPTE (EDS) Human consequences of crowding Plenum, 241-249.

HAMNETT, C. (1979) Area based explanations : a critical appraisal. In HERBERT, D.T. & D.M. SMITH (EDS) Social problems and the city Oxford Univ. Press, 244-260.

HARRIS, B. (1959) Urbanization policy in India Paps. & Procs. Reg. Sci. Assoc., 5, 181 - 203.

HART, H.C. (1960) Urban politics in Bombay : the meaning of community Economic Weekly , 983-988.

HILLERY, G. (1955) Definitions of community - areas of agreement Rural Sociol., 20, 111-123.

HOLLNSTEINER, M.R. (1977) People power : community participation in the planning of human settlements Assignment Children, 40, 11-47.

HOSELITZ, B.F. (1960) Urbanization in India Kyklos, 13, 361-370.

168

(1962) The role of urbanization
in economic development. In TURNER, R.
(ED) India's urban future Univ. California
Press, 157-176.
Reprinted in DWYER, D.J. (ED) (1974) The
city in the third world Macmillan, 168-
190.

INDIAN OXYGEN LIMITED (1973) India : a
statistical outline Oxford & I.B.H.
Publishing Co.

IYENGAR, S.K. (1957) Socio-economic survey of
Hyderabad-Secunderabad city area
Government Press, Hyderabad.

JAGMOHAN (1975) Rebuilding Shahjahanabad : the
walled city of Delhi Vikas.
(1978) Island of truth Vikas.

JAIN, S.P. (1975a) Panchayati raj in
Maharashtra Community Development &
Panchayati Raj Digest, 6, 177-189.
(1975b) The social structure of
Hindu-Muslim community National.

JAKOBSEN, L. & V. PRAKASH (1967) Urbanization
and regional planning in India Urban
Affairs Quart., 2, 36-65.
(EDS) (1971) Urbanization
and national development .
Vol. 1 : South and Southeast Asia urban
affairs annuals Sage.

JANAKI, V.A. & Z.A. SAYED (1962) The geography
of Padra town Baroda.

JANOWITZ, M. (1951) The community press in an
urban setting Free Press.

JONES, R.W. (1974) Urban politics in India
Univ. California Press.

JOSHI, H. (1976) Prospects and case
for employment of women in Indian cities
Econ.& Polit. Weekly, 11
& V. JOSHI (1976) Surplus labour and
the city : a study of Bombay Oxford Univ.
Press, Bombay.

KAR, N.R. (1963) Economic character of
metropolitan sphere of influence of
Calcutta Geogr. Rev. of India, 25, 108-137.

KARAN, P.P. (1957) The pattern of Indian towns :
a study in urban morphology Journ. Amer.
Inst. Planns. , 23, 70-75.
& W.A. BLADEN (1976) Geographical
aspects of environmental pollution in
India Geoforum, 7, 51-57.

KARPAT, K.H. (1976) The Gecekondu : rural
migration and urbanization Cambridge Univ.
Press.

KATAKAM, R. (1973) Urban strategy Hyderabad : a
case study Design, 17(6), 26-30.

KEENAN, J.L. (1935) A steel man in India
Gollancz.

KENNEDY, J.P. (1966) A report on the urban
community development projects in Delhi
and Ahmedabad Ford Foundation, New Delhi.

KHAN, W. (1967) Metropolitan Hyderabad : a
socio-economic profile Unpub. pap.
(1978a) Hyderabad : a bi-nuclear
metropolis Mimeo, unedited version of
Khan (1978b)

(1978b) Hyderabad : a bi-nuclear
metropolis. In MISRA, R.P. (ED) Million
cities of India Vikas, 182-212.
(1978c) Personal interview Director,
Administrative Staff Training College,
Hyderabad.
& K.N. GOPI (1968) Two suggestions on
the approach to the study of urban
population density patterns Pap. presented
at I.G.U. Symposium on Quantative
Geography, Univ. Mysore, Karnataka.

KHATU, K.K. (1977) Project on 'urban community
development to raise levels of
disadvantaged groups in Baroda'.Report
Baroda Citizens Council.
(1978a) Slums : a political
dimension and improvement strategy Quart.
Journ. Local Self-Government Institute
(Bombay), 60, 25-27.
(1978b) Squatters/hutments in
Baroda Vadodara Vikas, 11.
(1978c) Personal interviews
Executive Director, Baroda Citizens
Council.

KING, A.D. (1976) Colonial urban development :
culture, social power and environment
Routledge & Kegan Paul.

KINSLEY, G.T. & F.S. KRISTOFF (1971) A housing
policy for metropolitan Calcutta Calcutta
Metropolitan Planning Organisation.

KULKARNI, V.M. (1972) Role of municipal
government in social welfare services
Nagarlok, 4(4), 9-15.

LAKDAWALA, D.T. ET AL (1963) Work, wages and
well-being in an Indian metropolis :
economics survey of Bombay city Univ.
Bombay, Sers. in Economics No. 11.

LAL, A. (1958) Some characteristics of Indian
cities of over 100,000 inhabitants in
1951, with special reference to their
occupational structure and functional
specialization Unpub. Ph.D. Indiana Univ.
(1962) Age and sex structure of cities
of India Geogr. Rev. of India, 24, 7-29.

LAL, H. (1967) An experiment in
decentralization of municipal
administration Delhi Municipal Corporation.

LAMBERT, R.D. (1962) The impact of urban society
upon village life. In TURNER, R. (ED)
India's urban future Univ. California
Press, 117-140.

(1963) Workers, factories and social change in India Princeton Univ. Press.

LEARMONTH, A.T.A. (1973) Towards a spatial model of the South Asian city. In OPEN UNIVERSITY, The process of urbanization O.U. Press, 69-108.

LEARMONTH, A.T.A. & L.S. BHAT ((EDS) (1962) Mysore State : Vol. I Atlas of resources Indian Statistical Institute & Asia Publishing House, Calcutta.

LEARMONTH, A.T.A. ET AL (1962) Mysore State : Vol. II A regional synthesis Indian Statistical Institute & Asia Publishing House.

LIBBEE, M.J. & D.E. SOPHER (1975) Marriage migration in rural India. In KOSINKI, L.A. & R.M. PROTHERO (EDS) People on the move Methuen, 347-359.

LLOYD, P. (1979) Slums of hope? Penguin.

LUBELL, H. (1977) Migration and employment : the case of Calcutta Social Action, 27, 279-291.

LYNCH, O.M. (1967) Rural cities in India : continuities and discontinuities. In MASON, P. (ED) India and Ceylon : unity and diversity Oxford Univ. Press.
             (1969) The politics of untouchability : social mobility and social change in a city of India Columbia Univ. Press.

MADDICK, H. (1970) Panchayati raj Longman.

MAHADEVAN, M. (1977) Les creches mobiles en Inde Assignment children, 40, 68-86.

MAJUMDAR, D.N. (1958) Caste and communication in an Indian village Asia Publishing House.
             (1960) Social contours of an industrial city : social survey of Kanpur Asia Publishing House.

MAJUMDAR, T.K. (1977) The urban poor and social change : a study of squatter settlements in Delhi Social Action, 27, 216-240.

MALENBAUM, W. (1957) Urban unemployment in India Pacific Affairs, 30, 138-150.

MALHOTRA, P.C. (1964) Socio-economic survey of Bhopal city and Bairagarh New York.

MALIK, R.A. (1965) Cities of the upper Indo-Gangetic plain Pakistan Geogr. Journ. 10, 61-72.

MALKANI, H.C. (1957) A socio-economic survey of Baroda city Baroda.

MARRIOTT, McK. (ED) (1958) Village India Chicago Univ. Press.

MATHUR, J.S. (1956) A note on urban community projects in India and the second five year plan Delhi School of Social Work, mimeo.

MATHUR, M.N. (1959) Study of local bodies inside and at the periphery of Delhi state Planning Admin. Section, Town Planning Organisation, Delhi.

MAYER, A. (1956) Urban community development projects in India : some preliminary notes and questions Mimeo.

(1959) Pilot project India : the story of rural development at Etawah, Uttar Pradesh Univ. California Press.

McGEE, T.G. (1976) The persistence of the proto-proletariat Progr. in Geogr., 9, 1-38.

MEHTA, S.K. (1968) Patterns of residence in Poona (India) by income, education and occupation (1937-65) Amer. Journ. Sociol., 73, 496-508. Reprinted in SCHWIRIAN, K.P. (ED) (1974) Comparative urban structure D.C. Heath, 398-412.
(1969) Patterns of residence in Poona, India, by caste and religion : 1882-1965 Demography, 6, 473-491. Reprinted in SCHWIRIAN, K.P. (ED) (1974) Comparative urban structure, D.C. Heath, 492-512.

MENAFEE, A. (1971) Voluntary associations in a neighbourhood of New Delhi Pap. presented at meeting of Association for Asian studies.

MILNER, D. (1968) Calcutta - a city in despair Geogr. Mag., 41(1), 35-49.

MISRA, B.R. (1959) Report on socio-economic survey of Jamshedpur city Patna.

MISRA, R.P. (1978) Million cities of India Vikas.

MITRA, S. (1961) The future of population, urbanization and working force in India Univ. Chicago, Dept. Sociol., unpub. Ph.D.

MITRA, A. (1964) A functional classification of India's towns Institute of Economic Growth, New Delhi.
(1968) Delhi - capital city CFPI Reprography Unit, New Delhi.

MITTAL, A. (1971) Patterns of interaction and group formation in a government employees' colony in Delhi Sociol.Bull., 20, 39-53.

MOHSIN, M. (1964) Chittaranjan : a study in urban sociology Bombay.

MOOKHERJEE, D. & R.L. MORRILL (1973) Urbanization in a developing economy : Indian perspectives and patterns Sage.

MUKERJEE, R. & B. SINGH (1961) Social profiles of a metropolis : social and economic

structure of Lucknow, capital of Uttar Pradesh New York.
(1965) A district town in transition : social and economic survey of Gorakhpur Asia Publishing House.

MUNICIPAL CORPORATION OF DELHI, DEPARTMENT OF COMMUNITY DEVELOPMENT (1965) Second evaluation study of Vikas Mandals MCD.

MUNICIPAL CORPORATION OF HYDERABAD (1977) Habitat Hyderabad : East Lions Nagar MCH.

(1978) Habitat Hyderabad Mimeo
(n.d.) Better life through voluntary community effort MCH.

MURPHEY, R. (1964) The city in the swamp : aspects of the site and early growth of Calcutta Geogr. Journ. , 126, 241-256.

NANGIA, S. (1976) Delhi metropolitan region : a study in settlement geography K.B. Publications, New Delhi.

NATIONAL COUNCIL OF APPLIED ECONOMIC RESEARCH (1965) Market towns and spatial development in India NCAER, New Delhi. (1973) Techno-economic survey of Delhi NCAER.

NATIONAL INSTITUTE OF COMMUNITY DEVELOPMENT (1972) Micro-level planning Behavioural Sciences & Community Development, 6, 143-157.

NEALE, W.C. (1965) India: the search for unity, democracy and progress Van Nostrand.

NELSON, J. (1970) The urban poor : disruption or political integration in third world cities World Politics, 22, 393-414.

NILSSON, S. (1973) New Capitals of India, Pakistan and Bangladesh Scandinavian Institute of Asian Studies, Monograph 12.

NOBLE, A.G. & A.K. DUTT (1977) Indian urbanization and planning : vehicles of modernization Tata McGraw-Hill.

OLDENBURG, P. (1976) Big city government in India Univ. Arizona Press.

PANJABI, R.M. (1958) Chandigarh : India's newest city Geogr. Mag, 31, 401-414.

PARTHASARATHY, R & K.K. Khatu (1978) Urban development and urban authorities Nagarlok, 10, 44-60.

PAYNE, G.K. (1977) Urban housing in the third world Leonard Hill.

PRAKASH, V. (1969) New towns in India Duke Univ., Monograph 8.

RAJ, D. (1972) Administrative organisation for social welfare at the local level Nagarlok, 4, 24-30.
(1978) Million cities of India : planning and administration. In MISRA, R.P. (ED) Million cities of India Vikas, 322-345.

RAJAGOPALAN, C. (1962) The Greater Bombay : a study in suburban ecology Bombay.

RAO, D.V.R. & H.P. BHARI (1972) An urban renewal study of Motia Khan, Delhi Urban & Rural Plann. Thought, 15, 48-92.

RAO, K.R. & K.R. MURTHY (1972) Cultural matrix and reference group behaviour : the case of Desanskritization and Islamization of the Telangana Brahmins Anthropologist, 25, 241-247.

RAO, P.V. (1972) Social welfare services in municipal corporations : a survey Nagarlok, 4(4), 16-23.

RAO, S. (1978) Personal interview Director, Municipal Corporation of Hyderabad, Urban Community Development Department.

RAO, V.K.V.R. & P.B. DESAI (1965) Greater Delhi : a study in urbanisation - 1940-1957 Asia Publishing House.

RAO, V.L.S.P. (1964) The towns of Mysore state Indian Statistical Institute & Asia Publishing House.
& L.S. BHAT (1960) Regional planning in the Mysore state - the need for readjustment of district boundaries Indian Statistical Institute.
& R. RAMACHANDRAN (1975) A report on the socio-economic survey of Vijaywada city Univ. of Delhi, Dept. of Human Geog.
& V.K. TEWARI (1976) Bangalore : an emerging metropolis Institute for Social & Economic Change, Human Geog. & Ecology Unit, Bangalore.
(1978) Urbanisation in India : spatial dimensions Institute for Social & Economic Change, Bangalore.

RESEARCH & EVALUATION UNIT, DEPARTMENT OF URBAN COMMUNITY DEVELOPMENT, MUNICIPAL CORPORATION OF DELHI (1961) Evaluation study of the formation and working of Vikas Mandals : 'citizens development councils' MCD, mimeo.

RICHARDS, S.F. (1972) Geographic mobility of industrial workers in India : a case study of four factory labour forces. In DWYER, D.J. (ED) The city as a centre of change in Asia Hong Kong Univ. Press, 72-95.

RIDKER, R.R. & H. LUBELL (EDS) (1971) Employment and unemployment of the near east and South Asia. Vol. I : Delhi New York.

RIFKIN, S.B. (1977) Community health in Asia
    Christian Conference of Asia.

ROSSER, C. (1971) Housing for the lowest income
    groups - the Calcutta experience Ekistics,
    31(183), 126-131.

ROWE, W.L. (1973) Caste, kinship and
    association in urban India. In SOUTHALL,
    A. (ED) Urban anthropology Oxford Univ.
    Press, 211-250.

RUDOLPH, L.I. & S.H. RUDOLPH (1960) The
    political role of India's caste
    associations Pacific Affairs, 33, 5-22.

SAXENA, D.P. (1977) Rururban migration in India
    : causes and consequences Popular
    Prakashan.

SCOTTISH DEVELOPMENT DEPARTMENT (1974)
    Community councils : some alternatives
    for community council schemes in Scotland
    H.M.S.O.

SELBOURNE, D. (1977) An eye to India Penguin.

SEN, S.N. (1960) The city of Calcutta : a
    socio-economic survey , 1954-5 to 1957-8
    Firma Mukhopadhyay, Calcutta.

SETHURAMAN, S.V. (1976) The urban informal
    sector : concept, measurement and policy
    Internatl. Labour Rev., 114, 75-76.

SHAH, K. (1977) Housing for the urban poor in
    Ahmedabad : an integrated urban development
    approach Social Action, 27, 335-352.

SHAH, S.M. (1974) Growth centres as a strategy
    for rural development : Indian experience
    Economic Development & Cultural Change,
    22, 215-218.

SHARMA, O.P. (1975) Operational structure of
    urban working women The Economic Times ,
    June 15th.

SINGH, A.M. (1976) Neighbourhood and social
    networks in urban India : south Indian
    voluntary associations in Delhi Marwah,
    New Delhi.
        (1977) Women and the family :
    coping with poverty in the bastis of
    Delhi Social Action , 27, 241-265.
        (1978a) Rural-urban migration of
    women among the urban poor in India :
    causes and consequences Social Action ,
    28, 326-356.
        (1978b) Slum and pavement dwellers
    in urban India : some urgent research and
    policy considerations Social Action , 28,
    164-187.
        (1978c) Personal communications
    Consultant to the Social Development
    Branch of the United Nations, and Indian
    Social Institute.
        & A. de SOUZA (1977) Slum and
    pavement dwellers in the major cities of
    India social situation rep. submitted to

the Dept. of Social Work, Government of India.

SINGH, J. (1979) Central place hierarchy in a backward economy : Gorakhpur region (India) Tijds. Econ. & Soc. Geogr. , 70, 300-306.

SINGH, R.L. (1955) Banaras : a study in urban geography Nand Kishore & Bros., Banaras.
        (1964) Bangalore - an urban study The National Geographical Society of India. Varanasi.
        (ED) (1968) India : regional studies Calcutta.

SINGH, U. (1959) New Delhi : its site and situation National Geogr. Journ. of India, 5.

        (1961) Allahabad : a study in urban geography Varanasi.

SINHA, G.P. & S.N. RANADE (1975) Women construction workers : reports of two surveys Indian Council for Social Science Research.

SIVARAMAKRISHNAN, K.C. (1977a) Slum improvement in Calcutta Assignment Children, 40, 87-115.
                (1977b) The slum improvement programme in Calcutta : the role of the CMDA Social Action, 27, 292-305.

SMAILES, A.E. (1969) The Indian city : a descriptive model Geographische Zeitschrift, 57, 177-190.

SOVANI, N.V. (1966) Urbanization and urban India Asia Publishing House.
        ET AL (1956) Poona: a re-survey: the changing pattern of employment and earnings Gokhale Institute of Politics & Economics, Pune, Pub. No. 34.

SPATE, O.H.K. (1956) Two federal capitals - New Delhi and Canberra Geographical Outlook (India) , 1, 1-8.
        & E. AHMAD (1950) Five cities of the Indo-Gangetic plain Geogl.Rev., 40, 260-278.
        & A.T.A. LEARMONTH (1967) India and Pakistan Methuen, 3rd. ed.

SUNDARAM, K.V. (1978) Delhi : the national capital. In MISRA, R.P. (ED) Million cities of India Vikas, 105-154.

TANEJA, K. (1971) Morphology of Indian cities National Geographical Society of India.

TANGRI, S.S. (1968) Urban growth, housing and economic development : the case of India Asian Survey, 8, 519-538.

TEWARI, V.K. (1978) A model of Bangalore metropolis Institute for Social & Economic Change, Bangalore.

THACKER, M.S. (1965) India's urban problem
    Univ. of Mysore.

THAKORE, M.P. (1962) Aspects of the urban
    geography of New Delhi Univ. London,
    unpub. Ph.D.

TOWN & COUNTRY PLANNING ORGANISATION (1975)
    Jhuggi jhompri settlements in Delhi :
    a sociological study of low-income
    migrant communities Town & Country
    Planning Division, Ministry of Works &
    Housing, Government Of India. Mimeo.

TURNER, R. (ED) (1962) India's urban future
    Univ..California Press.

TURNER, J.F.C. (1966) Uncontrolled urban
    settlement : problems and policies
    Univ. Pittsburgh, Wkng. Pap. 11.
    Reprinted in BREESE , G. (1972) The city
    in newly developing countries Prentice-
    Hall, 507-534.

ULACK, R. (1978) The role of urban squatter
    settlements Annals Assoc. Amer. Geogrs.,
    68, 535-550.

UNITED NATIONS (1974) World housing survey U.N.
                DEPARTMENT OF ECONOMIC &
    SOCIAL AFFAIRS (1976) Poverty,
    unemployment and development policy : a
    case study of selected issues with
    reference to Kerala U.N.

VATUK, S. (1972) Kinship and urbanization :
    white collar migrants in North India
    Univ. California Press.

VENKATARAYAPPA, K.N. (1957) Bangalore :
    a socio-ecological study Univ. Bombay
    Press.

VENKATASUBBAN , A.V. (1958) Urban community
    development Ministry of Health,
    Government of India, mimeo.

WARD, P.M. (1976) Intra-city migration to
    squatter settlements in Mexico City
    Geoforum, 7, 369-382.
            (1978) Social interaction patterns
    in squatter settlements in Mexico City
    Geoforum, 9, 235-243.

WEINER, M. & J.O. FIELD (1970) India's urban
    constituencies Comparative Politics,
    8, 183-222.

WEINSTEIN, J.A. (1974) Madras : an anlysis of
    urban ecological structure in India Sage.
            & V.K. PILLAI (1979)
    Ahmedabad : an ecological perspective
    Third World Plann. Rev., 1, 205-233.

WERTHEIM, W.F. (1977) The integration of town
    and countryside in China Progr. in Plann.
    8, 163-170.

WEST BENGAL (1966) Basic development plan for
    the Calcutta Metropolitan District,
    1966-1986 Calcutta Metropolitan Planning

Organisation.

WIEBE, P.D. (1975) Social Life in an Indian
slum Vikas.
(1977) Interdependence not duality
: slum perspectives Social Action,
27, 206-215.

WIRSING, R.G. (1973) Associational 'micro -
arenas' in Indian urban politics Asian
Survey, April, 408-420.

WORLD BANK (1979) Annual Report .

YADAV, C.S. (1976) The spatial patterns of
residential land use structure in urban
Delhi Univ. Delhi, Dept. Geog., unpub.
Ph.D.

ZACHARIAH, K.C. (1966) Bombay migrational
study : a pilot analysis of migration to
an Asian metropolis Demography, 3,
378-392. Reprinted in BREESE, G. (ED)
(1972) The city in newly developing
countries Prentice-Hall, 360-375.

Index

S